Spiralizer Recipes

50 The Best Spiralizer Recipes From Classic Pasta Dishes, To Salads, Noodle Soups, Fries, Breakfast Noodles

Crush Your Pasta Cravings With Spiralizer Cookbook

Table Of Contents

Introduction

The spiralizer is a chef's dream and well kept secret, because it helps him or her create a wide variety of healthy meals with vegetable and fruit pasta and ribbons. With this cookbook, you can also prepare nutritious and incredibly healthy dishes, such as pasta dishes, soups, noodles, snacks, and even dessert!

In this book, you will find a guide on how to use your spiralizer effectively and choose the right ingredients to spiralize. You will also find some tips on how to choose the right spiralizer for your kitchen, if you do not have one yet.

Best of all, you can choose recipes from five chapters for your vegetable and fruit pastas, salads, soups, snacks and side dishes, and even sweets! The recipes in this ebook require ingredients that are affordable and easy to find. Most of the recipes are gluten free and rely on healthy herbs and spices as flavoring. This makes it a cookbook that is good for your health!

So who would benefit the most from this cookbook? Definitely those who want to lose weight, wish to start a healthier lifestyle, manage a health issue such as diabetes, heart disease, or allergies, and those who simply want to eat more vegetables everyday.

Thanks again for buying this book, I hope you enjoy it!

Chapter 1 - How to Use a Spiralizer

Traditional pasta, which is made from wheat and other grains, may be delicious and quite addictive, but it can also be unhealthy if eaten too often and too much. Fortunately, you can still enjoy an alternative kind of pasta on a regular basis, which is made of vegetables with the help of a spiralizer.

What is a Spiralizer?

A spiralizer is a kitchen tool that will easily process fresh vegetables into a noodle form. Many restaurants, especially those which cater to those who follow the raw diet, make use of the spiralizer to create and sell healthy and delicious food. However, you can enjoy your own homemade spiralized dishes as the typical spiralizer is quite affordable, with the average price at about 40 US dollars, and it is fairly easy to use, not unlike a mechanical pencil sharpener. To use it, one simply places a vegetable in a clamp on top of the grinder, then turn the handle crank to process the vegetable into ribbons that resemble cooked pasta.

One great benefit of having a spiralizer is that you can add more vegetables into your dishes quite easily. Those who want to lose weight or improve their health can prepare vegetable dishes effortlessly at home. People who are sensitive to gluten will also greatly benefit from the spiralizer since they will be able to enjoy more types of dishes by following traditional recipes but with the spiralized substitutes.

To choose a spiralizer for your kitchen, find one that is safe to use. Make sure to get a model that will not necessitate you to touch the blades at all as you spiralize. Some models have a handle or safety guard feature to keep you from doing so. Another factor is speed. Find a spiralizer that can quickly turn your vegetables into pasta quickly and easily. Uniformity of the noodles should also be considered. Finally, find a spiralizer that is easy to clean. You will find that you will not be able to use your spiralizer as often as you would like if it is a pain to clean afterward.

The Different Types of Spiralizers

There are quite a number of spiralizer brands out there nowadays. All you have to do now is to browse through reviews online to find the one that best suits your budget and lifestyle.

The cheapest spiralizer is the hand held type, and it looks like a large pencil sharpener. If you only wish to spiralizer carrots, cucumbers, and zucchini, then you will find this to be good enough.

The second model is the tabletop spiralizer, and it comes with at least three kinds of blades. The first blade will give you corkscrew noodles, the second would be spiral ribbons, and the third will let you create spaghetti-like strands. It is the most popularly used spiralizer in the home.

The Best Ingredients to Spiralize

You can spiralize almost any kind of whole food that is suited to the functionality of the spiralizer, but if you do not know which one to choose next, then let this list help you out:

- Apple: to spiralize apples, it is best to choose organic ones that are firm and have no soft spots. You can remove the core, but it is advised that you do not peel to give your apple ribbons more color.

- Beet: since beets are quite hard, you can slice the beet that you wish to spiralize into 2 inch lengths first.

- Bell pepper: remove the stem and core of the bell peppers before inserting them into the spiralizer.

- Broccoli: peel the hard outer skin of the broccoli stalks before inserting into the spiralizer. It is recommended that you blanch the stalks before serving.

- Cabbage: the spiralizer can shred the cabbage leaves more quickly compared to using a knife. Rinse well, slice into the right shape for the spiralizer, then process.

- Carrot: peel and remove the greens, then spiralize.

- Celeriac: simply rinse and spiralize.

- Chayote squash: rinse, peel, and spiralize.

- Cucumber: peeled or unpeeled, firm cucumbers can be spiralized quite easily.

- Eggplant: choose a spiralizer that can produce flat ribbons to spiralize eggplants. Make sure to drain and cook the eggplants before serving.

- Jerusalem artichoke: can easily be spiralized. Best served cooked.

- Jicama or yam bean: slice into more manageable pieces before spiralizing. Can be served raw.

- Leek: quick and easy to spiralize. Best served blanched with salt and olive oil.

- Onion: can be sliced into uniform rings.

- Parsnip: slice into smaller pieces first before spiralizing. Best served baked or roasted.

- Pear: remove the stem and core, then quarter before spiralizing.

- Plantain: can easily be spiralized due to firmness.

- Potato: small potatoes can be spiralized to make noodles or fries. Boil potatoes before spiralizing.

- Pumpkin: remove the seeds and slice into smaller pieces before spiralizing.

- Radish: slice into ribbons quickly with a spiralizer. Can be served raw.

- Squash: peel, remove the seeds, and spiralize.

- Sweet potato: peel and slice into 2 inch thick pieces first before spiralizing as it is a hard vegetable. Always cook before serving.

- Turnip: this dense vegetable should be sliced into 2 inch pieces before spiralizing.

- Yam: the density of this vegetable requires a high quality spiralizer to turn it into ribbons or strips.

- Zucchini: can easily be spiralized peeled or not. Choose the straight and thick ones.

How to Prepare the Vegetable Pasta

You can choose to serve most vegetables raw or blanched. The three vegetables that should always be blanched before serving are eggplants, sweet potatoes, and potatoes, because they contain certain bacteria that will be harmful to your digestive tract if not cooked beforehand.

To blanch your vegetable pasta, you can choose to microwave them for 10 seconds or more in a bowl of water to tenderize. You can also boil some water, turn off the heat, and then plunge the pasta into the hot water and keep them there for 30 seconds or more. After that, drain the pasta and set aside. To preserve crispness, you can immediately plunge them in ice water to stop the cooking process.

Vegetable pasta can also be sautéed or stir fried along with the other ingredients in the recipe. You can also bake them to make them crisp on the outside but tender on the inside.

Also, if you have any leftover vegetable pasta, you can still store them (for up to 24 hours for raw and up to 48 hours for blanched) by placing them in an airtight glass or plastic container, then putting them in the coldest shelf inside your fridge. For best results, add freshly squeezed lemon juice to the pasta before storing.

Chapter 2 - Pasta Recipes

Lemon and Ricotta Veggie Pasta

Number of Servings: 1 serving

Ingredients:

- 2 cups yellow squash or zucchini pasta

- 4 cups water

- 4 oz ricotta cheese

- 2 Tbsp butter

- 1/4 cup chopped flat leaf parsley

- 1/4 tsp black pepper

- Zest of 1/2 lemon

Instructions:

1. Boil the water in a saucepan, then add the pasta. Cook for 1 minute or until all dente. Drain the pasta and plunge in ice water. Drain and place in a bowl.

2. Take 1/2 cup of boiling water and pour into a saucepan. Add the butter and cheese and stir until thickened.

3. Add the sauce into the bowl and toss in the lemon zest, pepper, and parsley. Mix carefully, then serve.

Vegetable Lasagna

Number of Servings: 3

Ingredients:

- 3 medium, extra firm eggplants, spiralized into spiral ribbons

- 1 Tbsp sea salt

- 2 Tbsp olive oil

- 1 small red onion, diced

- 2 garlic cloves

- 1/2 tsp dried basil

- 1/2 tsp dried oregano

- 1/4 tsp dried thyme

- 1/2 cup red wine

- 4 oz canned tomatoes

- 1/2 Tbsp tomato paste

- 1/2 yellow onion, diced

- 4 oz button or cremini mushrooms, sliced

- 1 large zucchini, spiralized into ribbons

- 1 yellow squash, spiralized into thick ribbons

- 1/2 fennel bulb

- 2 cups baby spinach leaves

- 4 oz fresh mozzarella

- 4 oz ricotta cheese

- 1/4 cup freshly grated Parmesan cheese

Instructions:

1. Place the eggplant ribbons into a colander and season with salt. Toss carefully to coat, then set aside for 30 minutes.

2. Place a saucepan over medium flame and heat 1/2 tablespoon of the olive oil. Stir in the red onion and cook until caramelized. Stir in the dried herbs and garlic and cook for 1 minute.

3. Pour the wine into the saucepan and cook until wine is reduced to half. Stir in the tomato paste and tomatoes. Partially cover and let simmer for 15 minutes.

4. Turn off the heat and set aside to cool.

5. Place another saucepan over medium flame and heat 1/2 tablespoon of olive oil. Stir in the yellow onion and cook until translucent. Stir in the mushrooms and season with salt. Cook until mushrooms are browned.

6. Scrape the sautéed mushrooms into a plate and set aside to cool.

7. Using the same saucepan, heat the remaining olive oil over medium flame. Add the spinach and season with salt. Cook until wilted, then turn off the heat and set aside to cool.

8. Rinse the eggplant ribbons and carefully pat dry. Spiralize the squash, fennel, and zucchini into flat ribbons.

9. Set the oven to 375 degrees F to preheat. Coat a baking dish with nonstick cooking spray.

10. Pour the tomato sauce into the baking dish, then add half each of the zucchini, followed by the fennel, spinach, ricotta, eggplant ribbons, mushrooms, and finally the mozzarella. Repeat with the remaining half.

11. Top the dish with Parmesan cheese, cover with aluminum foil, and bake for 25 minutes.

12. Carefully take off the aluminum cover and bake for 5 minutes, or until top is golden brown. Serve at once.

Zucchini Pasta with Eggplant Sauce

Number of Servings: 1

Ingredients:

- 2 cups zucchini pasta

- 2 small eggplants, peeled and diced

- 1 small yellow onion, chopped

- 14 oz Italian style plum tomatoes

- 2 garlic cloves, minced

- 2 oz canned sliced mushrooms, drained

- 2 1/2 Tbsp dry red wine

- 2 1/2 Tbsp water

- 3/4 tsp Italian seasoning

- 1 Tbsp pitted and sliced black olives

Instructions:

13. In a pot, combine the eggplants, onion, tomatoes, garlic, mushrooms, wine, and water. Cover over lowest possible heat setting for 1 hour, or until ingredients are very tender.

14. In a saucepan, boil 2 cups of water and blanch the zucchini pasta. Drain and transfer into a bowl.

15. Add the Italian seasoning and olives into the eggplant mixture and mix well. Pour the sauce over the pasta and serve at once.

Mexican Mac and Cheese

Number of Servings: 3

Ingredients:

- 1 cup yellow squash or zucchini flat circle noodles

- 1/2 lb ground turkey or beef

- 1 small bell pepper, seeded and diced

- 1/2 package taco seasoning mix

- 8 oz canned Mexican style stewed tomatoes

- 1/4 cup water

- 1 cup shredded Cheddar cheese

Instructions:

1. Set the oven to 375 degrees F to preheat.

2. Place a greased skillet over medium flame and cook the onion, bell pepper, and ground turkey or beef until meat is browned and cooked through.

3. Add the water and canned tomatoes with their juices into the skillet, then mix well. Stir in the taco seasoning mix and let it simmer for 5 minutes.

4. Lightly grease a baking dish with nonstick cooking spray or butter, then pour in half of the

meat mixture, followed by half the squash or zucchini noodles, then half the cheese. Repeat the same sequence.

5. Bake for 3 minutes in the oven, or until cheese is melted. Serve at once.

Dilled Salmon Pasta

Number of Servings: 1

Ingredients:

- 2 cups yellow squash or zucchini noodles, blanched
- 2 oz smoked salmon, sliced thinly
- 1/4 cup dry white wine
- 2 Tbsp chopped fresh dill
- 1/2 small red onion, minced
- 1 1/2 Tbsp olive oil
- 1/4 cup freshly squeezed lemon juice
- 4 oz frozen peas, thawed and drained
- 1/2 lemon, sliced into wedges

Instructions:

1. Place a skillet over medium flame and heat the oil. Add the onion and saute until translucent.

2. Stir in the white wine and let simmer until liquids reduce to half. Add the dill and salmon and let simmer until sauce thickens.

3. Place the veggie pasta into a bowl and pour the sauce on top. Toss to coat, then serve at once with lemon wedges.

Puttanesca

Number of Servings: 1

Ingredients:

- 2 cups yellow squash or zucchini spaghetti pasta, raw or blanched

- 3 anchovies in oil

- 14 oz canned crushed tomatoes

- 1/4 cup chopped pitted black olives

- 1 Tbsp tomato paste

- 2 garlic cloves, minced

- 1/2 tsp crushed red pepper flakes

- 1/2 Tbsp Italian seasoning

- 1/4 small yellow onion, minced

Instructions:

1. Place a skillet over medium high flame and heat the olive oil. Add the onions and sauté until translucent. Stir in the garlic and anchovies. Cook until anchovies melt.

2. Stir in the crushed tomatoes with their juices, tomato paste, red pepper flakes, olives, and Italian seasoning.

3. Set heat to low and let simmer for 8 minutes.

4. Place the pasta on a plate and pour the sauce on top. Toss gently to coat, then serve.

Anchovy and Zucchini Pasta

Number of Servings: 3

Ingredients:

- 2 cups zucchini noodles, raw

- 6 anchovy fillets in olive oil, drained

- 1/2 cup olive oil

- 1/2 Tbsp crushed red pepper flakes

- Juice of 1/2 lemon

- 2 Tbsp chopped fresh flat leaf parsley

Instructions:

1. Place a saucepan over medium flame and heat the olive oil. Add the minced anchovies and cook until fish is thoroughly combined with the oil.

2. Add the red pepper flakes and stir until fragrant. Add the lemon juice and stir to combine.

3. Pour the sauce over the zucchini noodles and toss gently to coat. Serve at once.

Squash Pasta with Bacon and Tomato

Number of Servings: 1

Ingredients:

- 1 cup yellow squash flat circle noodles
- 1/2 cup halved cherry tomatoes
- 2 strips chopped thick cut bacon
- 1 small red onion, minced
- 2 garlic cloves, minced
- 1/4 cup white wine
- 3/4 cup chicken broth
- 1/4 cup chopped fresh arugula
- 1 1/2 Tbsp olive oil
- 1 Tbsp Italian seasoning

Instructions:

1. Place a skillet over medium flame and cook the bacon until crisp. Transfer the bacon onto a plate lined with paper towels. Drain most of the grease.

2. Add the onion into the skillet and cook until translucent, then stir in the garlic and cook until fragrant.

3. Add the white wine and scrape the browned bits from the bottom. Stir in the tomatoes and chicken stock. Bring to a simmer, then stir in the Italian seasoning.

4. Crumble the crisp bacon and stir into the skillet. Stir in the yellow squash noodles and mix well.

5. Stir in the arugula and cook until wilted, then transfer to a plate and serve.

Turkey and Potato Pasta

Number of Servings: 2

Ingredients:

- 2 cups potato ribbons, blanched
- 3/4 lb ground turkey
- 1 small yellow onion, chopped
- 2 garlic cloves, minced
- 2 1/2 Tbsp dry red wine
- 14.5 oz Italian style diced tomatoes
- 1 small carrot, chopped
- 1 Tbsp Italian seasoning
- 2 1/2 Tbsp low fat cream
- 1 Tbsp olive oil
- Parmesan cheese

Instructions:

1. Place a saucepan over medium flame and heat the oil. Stir in the onion, garlic, turkey and carrot. Cook until turkey is browned, then stir in the wine and cook until wine evaporates.

2. Add the tomatoes with juices, then the cream and Italian seasoning. Sauté to combine.

3. Set heat to low, cover the saucepan, and let simmer for about 15 minutes or until thickened.

4. Place the blanched potato ribbons into a bowl and ladle the soup on top. Sprinkle grated Parmesan cheese over the dish and serve at once.

Bacon and Ricotta Breakfast Noodles

Number of Servings: 2

Ingredients:

- 2 cups zucchini, spiralized into flat ribbons
- 1 slice bacon, chopped
- 1 small yellow onion, minced
- 1 small red bell pepper, diced
- 1 large garlic clove, crushed
- 14 oz canned diced tomatoes
- 1/4 cup ricotta cheese

Instructions:

1. Place a saucepan over medium flame and add the bacon. Cook until partially crisp, then drain most of the grease and stir in the onion and pepper. Cook until onion is translucent.

2. Stir in the garlic and cook until fragrant, then stir in the tomatoes with their juices. Let simmer for 10 minutes or until sauce thickens.

3. Stir in the cheese and cook until melted. Stir in the pasta and cook until tender. Serve at once.

Vegetable Bolognese

Number of Servings: 2

Ingredients:

- 1 Tbsp olive oil
- 1 celery stalk, diced
- 1/2 yellow onion, diced
- 1 medium carrot, diced
- 1/4 tsp dried basil
- 1/4 tsp dried oregano
- 1/8 tsp dried thyme
- 3 garlic cloves, minced
- 1 cup green lentils, rinsed
- 2 cups vegetable stock
- 6 oz canned crushed tomatoes
- 1 Tbsp tomato paste
- 1/4 tsp sea salt
- 1/4 tsp freshly ground black pepper
- 2 large zucchini squash
- 2 Tbsp chopped fresh flat leaf parsley
- 2 Tbsp freshly grated Parmesan cheese

Instructions:

1. Place a sauce pan over medium flame and heat half of the oil. Sauté the onion, carrot, celery, dried herbs, and half of the minced garlic. Cook until tender and fragrant.

2. Stir in the lentils and cook for 1 minutes. Stir in the stock, then increase heat to boiling. Reduce to a simmer and cook for 2c minutes or until lentils become tender.

3. Stir in the tomato paste and tomatoes, then let simmer for 10 minutes. Season to taste with salt and pepper.

4. Spiralize the zucchinis into spaghetti shreds. (C)A

5. Place a skillet over medium flame and heat the remaining oil. Saute the garlic and zucchini pasta with a dash of salt for 2 minutes. Transfer to a platter and ladle the sauce over the pile. Sprinkle cheese and parsley on top, then serve.

Chapter 3 - Salad Recipes

Greek Salad

Number of Servings: 3

Ingredients: (C)A

- 2 cups zucchini pasta, raw or blanched
- 1/2 bunch green onions, sliced
- 1 1/2 cups halved cherry tomatoes
- 1 cup sliced white mushrooms
- 1 small red bell pepper, seeded and julienned
- 2 oz pitted black olives
- 1/3 cup sliced pepperoni
- 1/2 cup crumbled feta cheese
- 1 large garlic clove, minced
- 1 tsp basil
- 3/4 tsp chopped fresh oregano
- 1/4 tsp black pepper
- 1/4 cup olive oil
- 1/4 cup red wine vinegar

Instructions:

1. In a salad bowl, gently toss together the zucchini pasta, green onion, cherry tomatoes, white mushrooms, bell pepper, and olives.

2. In a small jar, combine the basil, oregano, black pepper, olive oil, and red wine vinegar. Seal and shake vigorously to combine.

3. Drizzle the dressing all over the salad and toss carefully to coat. Arrange the pepperoni over the salad and sprinkle the feta cheese on top.

4. Cover and refrigerate for 3 to 12 hours to let the flavors combine. Serve chilled.

Jicama and Cilantro Salad

Number of Servings: 2 servings

Ingredients:

- 1 Tbsp olive oil
- Juice and zest of 1 lime
- 2 Tbsp agave nectar
- 1/2 red jalapeno chili, minced
- 1/4 tsp sea salt
- 1/4 tsp freshly ground black pepper
- 1 medium Jicama, spiralized into thin ribbons (A) ⬜
- 3 radishes, spiralized into ribbons
- 1 cup shredded green leaf or butter lettuce
- 1/2 cup whole cilantro leaves

Instructions:

1. In a salad bowl, whisk together the lime zest and juice, olive oil, jalapeno, agave nectar, salt, and pepper.

2. Add the Jicama ribbons into the bowl and toss gently to coat.

3. Add the radish ribbons and cilantro and toss again. Cover and chill for at least 1 hour.

4. Arrange the lettuce on a platter and chill for 1 hour. Heap the Jicama and cilantro salad on top of the lettuce. Serve chilled.

Mediterranean Salad

Number of Servings: 2

Ingredients:

- 2 cups zucchini ribbons, blanched or raw
- 1 cup cooked chicken breast, chopped
- 2 hard boiled eggs, diced
- 1 garlic clove, minced
- 1/2 small red onion, minced
- 1 1/2 Tbsp olive oil
- 1 Tbsp lemon juice
- 1/2 tsp chopped fresh basil
- 1/4 tsp dried rosemary
- 1 Tbsp chopped black olives

Instructions:

1. In a bowl, toss together the zucchini ribbons, diced hard boiled eggs, chicken, and red onion.

2. In a jar, combine the garlic, onion, olive oil, lemon juice, basil, and rosemary. Seal and shake vigorously to combine.

3. Drizzle the dressing all over the salad and toss carefully to coat. Top with chopped black olives and serve at once.

Balsamic Berry and Beet Salad

Number of Servings: 2

Ingredients:

- 2 beets, spiralized into shreds (C) △

- 1 small red onion, spiralized into shreds

- 2 Tbsp olive oil

- Juice and grated zest of 1/2 orange

- 1/2 Tbsp chopped fresh thyme leaves

- 1 Tbsp balsamic vinegar

- 1/4 tsp sea salt

- 1/4 tsp freshly ground black pepper

- 1/2 pint raspberries

- 1/2 pint blackberries

- 2 Tbsp chopped pistachios

Instructions:

1. Set the oven to 350 degrees F to preheat.

2. Place the spiralized beets in a bowl and add 1 tablespoon of olive oil. Toss to coat, then spread on a baking sheet and roast for 8 minutes, or until tender. Set on a wire rack to cool completely.

3. Place the onion shreds into a bowl of ice water and soak for 1 hour.

4. In a bowl, mix together the remaining olive oil, vinegar, thyme, orange juice and zest, and salt and pepper. Mix well, then toss in the roasted beet and onion shreds, and the berries.

5. Toss the salad carefully, then divide into 2 servings, sprinkle pistachios on top, and serve at once.

Vegetable and Hummus Salad

Number of Servings: 2

Ingredients:

(A)

- 2 cups zucchini ribbons, raw or blanched
- 1/2 cup carrot ribbons, raw or blanched
- 1/3 cup classic hummus
- 1/2 red bell pepper, seeded and diced
- 2 green onions, sliced thinly
- 2 Tbsp canola oil
- 1/2 tsp dark sesame oil
- 2 Tbsp soy sauce
- 2 Tbsp rice vinegar
- 1/2 tsp ground ginger
- 1 Tbsp chopped fresh mint
- 1/2 tsp crushed red pepper flakes

Instructions:

1. In a salad bowl, gently toss together the zucchini and carrot noodles with the green onion and pepper.

2. In a jar, mix together the canola and dark sesame oils, soy sauce, rice vinegar, ginger,

mint, and red pepper flakes. Seal and shake vigorously to combine.

3. Drizzle the dressing all over the salad and toss gently to coat. Drizzle the hummus on top and toss again. Serve at once.

Dilled Cucumber and Radish Salad

Number of Servings: 2

Ingredients:

- 1/2 cup sour cream
- 1/2 Tbsp dried dill weed
- 2 Tbsp minced fresh dill
- 2 Tbsp minced fresh chives or green onion
- Juice and grated zest of 1/2 lemon
- 1/4 tsp sea salt
- 1/4 tsp freshly ground black pepper
- 4 large red radishes, spiralized into ribbons
- 1 medium Persian or English cucumber, spiralized into ribbons

Instructions:

1. In a salad bowl, combine the dill weed, minced fresh dill, sour cream, chives, salt, pepper, and lemon zest and juice. Whisk well.

2. Toss the radish and cucumber ribbons into the bowl gently to coat. Chill for half an hour, then serve.

Thai Papaya Salad

Number of Servings: 2

Ingredients:

- 1 green papaya, peeled and spiralized into spaghetti (C) △

- 1 medium carrot, peeled and spiralized into spaghetti

- 1 cup bean sprouts

- 5 grape tomatoes, halved

- 1/4 cup chopped fresh basil

- 1/4 cup chopped unsalted peanuts

- 1 Tbsp canola oil

- 1/4 tsp soy sauce

- 1 Tbsp fish sauce

- Juice of 1 lime

Instructions:

1. In a salad bowl, toss together the papaya and carrot spaghetti with the bean sprouts, tomatoes, and basil.

2. In a bowl, whisk together the canola oil, soy and fish sauces, and lime juice. Drizzle on top of the salad and toss gently to coat.

3. Sprinkle the chopped peanuts on top and serve at once.

Waldorf Salad

Number of Servings: 2

Ingredients:

- 1/4 cup mayonnaise

- 1/8 tsp sea salt

- 1/4 tsp freshly ground black pepper

- 1 cup toasted chopped walnuts

- 1 celery stalk, diced

- 1 cup halved red and green grapes

- 2 Fuji apples, cored and spiralized into shreds (C)A

- Juice and grated zest of 1/2 lemon

Instructions:

1. In a bowl, whisk together the lemon juice and zest with the mayonnaise, salt and pepper.

2. Fold in the grapes, celery, and walnuts. Mix well.

3. Add the apple shreds into the mixture and toss to coat evenly. Cover the bowl and refrigerate for half an hour, then serve chilled.

Chicken and Noodle Salad

Number of Servings: 2

Ingredients:

(A)

- 1 1/2 cups yellow squash or zucchini ribbons, raw or blanched

- 1 cup chopped cooked chicken breast

- 1/4 cup creamy peanut butter

- 1 1/2 Tbsp water

- 2 Tbsp soy sauce

- 1 1/2 Tbsp rice vinegar

- 1 Tbsp chili garlic sauce

- 1 Tbsp grated fresh ginger

- 1/2 Tbsp light brown sugar

- 1/2 bunch cilantro leaves, chopped

- 1/2 bunch green onions, sliced thinly

- 1 medium carrot, grated

- 1/2 bell pepper, seeded and julienned

Instructions:

1. In a salad bowl, toss together the vegetable ribbons, chopped chicken, bell pepper, carrots, green onions, and cilantro.

2. In a blender or food processor, mix together the soy sauce, peanut butter, chili garlic sauce, water, and brown sugar. Process until smooth, adding more water, if needed.

3. Drizzle the dressing on top of the salad and toss gently to coat. Cover and refrigerate for 1 hour before serving.

Rosemary, Raisin, Apple and Fennel Salad

Number of Servings: 2

Ingredients:

- 1 Tbsp olive oil

- 1/2 small yellow onion, minced

- 1 Tbsp finely minced fresh rosemary needles

- 1/2 Tbsp white wine or cider vinegar

- 1/4 tsp sea salt

- 1/4 tsp freshly ground black pepper

- 1 fennel bulb, spiralized into shreds

- 1 large Fuji apple, cored and spiralized into shreds

Instructions:

1. Place the golden raisins in a small bowl and add boiling water. Let stand for half an hour to plump up.

2. Place a saucepan over medium flame and heat the olive oil. Stir in the onion and rosemary. Sauté until onions become translucent. Transfer into a bowl and set aside to cool to room temperature.

3. Add the salt, pepper, and vinegar into the rosemary mixture, then toss in the shredded fennel and apple. Coat in the dressing well, then toss in the raisins. Cover and chill for 1 hour before serving.

Chapter 4 - Soup Recipes

Daikon Miso Soup

Number of Servings: 2

Ingredients:

- 6 oz block firm tofu, pressed and drained
- 1 1/2 cups water
- 1/4 cup dried wakame or nori seaweed, cut into thin strips
- 2 inch piece fresh ginger root, unpeeled, chopped
- 1 Tbsp loose leaf green tea
- 1 medium daikon radish, spiralized into shreds
- 1 medium carrot, spiralized into shreds
- 1/2 cup dashi
- 1/4 cup miso
- 1 green onion, chopped
- 1/2 cup edamame beans, shelled

Instructions:

1. Soak the seaweed in cold water for half an hour.

2. Boil the water in a soup pot, then remove from heat. Stir in the green tea and ginger. Set aside for half an hour.

3. Slice the tofu into cubes, then set aside. Drain the seaweed.

4. Strain the tea and boil the tea water in a small soup pot. Stir in the soaked seaweed and dashi. Cook for 3 minutes, then reduce to a simmer and stir in the miso until dissolves.

5. Stir in the carrots, daikon, green onion, tofu, and edamame. Cook for 2 minutes, then serve at once.

Black Bean and Squash Noodle Soup

Number of Servings: 3

Ingredients:

- 1 cup yellow squash noodles

- 7 oz vegetable broth

- 8 oz salsa

- 7 oz canned black beans, drained and rinsed

- 1 cup frozen corn kernels

- Juice of 1/2 lime

- 1 tsp chili powder

- 1/4 tsp cumin

Instructions:

1. Pour the broth into a saucepan and place over medium high flame. Bring to a boil, then reduce and let simmer.

2. Add the salsa, black beans, corn, and squash noodles. Cook for 1 minute.

3. Add the lime juice, chili powder and cumin. Stir gently, then cook for 1 minute.

4. Ladle into soup bowls and serve at once.

Shiitake Soba Noodle Soup

Number of Servings: 2

Ingredients:

- 3 cups dashi
- 4 pieces dried shiitake mushrooms
- 2 Tbsp miso
- 1/2 tsp grated fresh ginger root
- 1 small kohlrabi, spiralized into thick shreds
- 4 oz fresh shiitake mushrooms, sliced
- 1/2 tsp soy sauce or tamari
- 1 green onion, minced
- 1 cup baby bok choy, sliced thinly
- Bonito flakes
- Red pepper flakes
- Ponzu sauce

Instructions:

1. Place a soup pot over high flame and mix together the dried shiitake mushrooms and dashi. Bring to a boil, then reduce flame and let it simmer for 3 minutes or until mushrooms

become tender. Take the mushrooms out and set aside on a plate and slice.

2. Stir the ginger and miso into the soup pot, then the spiralized kohlrabi, and sliced re-hydrated shiitake mushrooms. Stir in the fresh mushrooms, green onion, bok choy, and tamari or soy sauce. Stir and let simmer until heated through.

3. Ladle into soup bowls and season with bonito flakes, red pepper flakes, and ponzu sauce.

Pumpkin Noodle Soup C △

Number of Servings: 3

Ingredients:

- 2 cups pumpkin noodles

- 2 1/2 cups vegetable broth

- 15 oz pumpkin puree

- 1 small yellow onion, minced

- 1 Tbsp olive oil

- 1/4 Tbsp brown sugar or granulated sugar substitute

- 1 tsp sage (or 1 Tbsp chopped fresh)

- 1/2 tsp cinnamon

- 1/8 tsp cayenne pepper

- 1/8 tsp ginger

- 1/16 tsp nutmeg

Instructions:

1. Place a soup pot over medium flame and heat the oil. Add the onion and cook until translucent, then add the cinnamon, cayenne, ginger, and nutmeg. Cook until fragrant.

2. Add the vegetable broth and pumpkin puree. Stir, then bring to a boil. Reduce heat to let simmer.

3. Add the sugar and stir until dissolved. Stir in the pumpkin noodles and cook for 2 minutes or until al dente.

4. Ladle into soup bowls and serve at once.

Beef and Noodle Soup

Number of Servings: 2

Ingredients:

- 1 Tbsp flour
- 1/2 tsp sea salt
- 1/4 tsp freshly ground black pepper
- 1 lb beef chuck, cubed
- 1 1/2 Tbsp unsalted butter
- 1/2 yellow onion, minced
- 1 celery stalk, diced
- 1/4 tsp dried oregano
- 1/4 tsp dried thyme
- 1 garlic clove, minced
- 1 cup red wine
- 3/4 quart beef or vegetable stock
- 1 small Russet potato
- 1 large carrot
- 1 small parsnip
- 1/2 kohlrabi
- 2 large kale leaves, chopped

- 1 1/2 Tbsp red wine vinegar

Instructions:

1. Rinse the beef cubes, then pat dry.

2. In a plate, combine the salt, pepper, and flour, then coat the beef cubes with the mixture.

3. Place a soup pot over medium flame and melt the butter. Stir in the onion, thyme, celery, oregano, and cook until onion becomes translucent.

4. Set heat to high and stir in the beef cubes. Cook until browned, then stir in the garlic stock, and water. Cover and bring to a boil, then reduce heat. Let simmer for 20 minutes, or until the beef is cooked through and tender.

5. Spiralize the carrot, potato, parsnip, and kohlrabi into ribbons, then add to the soup pot.

6. Let it simmer for 3 minutes, then stir in the chopped kale. Cook for 2 minutes, then stir in the red wine vinegar. Adjust seasoning to taste, then serve.

Beef Pho

Number of Servings: 2

Ingredients:

- 1 cup yellow squash noodles

- 4 cups low sodium beef broth

- 2 cups water

- 1/3 lb flank steak, sliced thinly

- 1 small yellow onion, sliced

- 3 garlic cloves, minced

- 1 inch piece fresh ginger root, grated

- 1 whole clove

- 1/2 cinnamon stick

- 1 Tbsp fish sauce

- Garnish: chopped green onion, lime wedges, chopped cilantro

Instructions:

1. In a soup pot, mix together the broth, water, garlic, ginger, whole clove, and cinnamon stick. Place over high flame, then bring to a boil. Reduce heat and cover. Let simmer for 20 minutes.

2. Stir in the beef and cook for 3 minutes or until beef is cooked through. Stir in the noodles and cook for 1 to 2 minutes.

3. Take out the cinnamon stick, ladle into soup bowls, top with garnish, and serve at once.

Vegetarian Minestrone

Number of Servings: 3

Ingredients:

- 1 Tbsp olive oil

- 1/2 yellow onion, diced

- 1 celery stalk, diced

- 1 garlic clove

- 1/2 Tbsp dried basil

- 1/2 Tbsp dried oregano

- 1/2 tsp dried thyme

- 1/2 cup red wine

- 7 oz canned crushed tomatoes

- 1/2 Tbsp tomato paste

- 2 1/2 cups vegetable stock

- 1 medium carrot

- 1 small parsnip

- 1/2 celery root

- 1/2 zucchini squash

- 4 oz canned kidney beans, rinsed and drained

- 4 oz canned white beans, rinsed and drained

- 1/2 tsp sea salt

- 1/4 tsp freshly ground black pepper

- 1 1/2 Tbsp red wine vinegar

- 2 Tbsp chopped fresh basil leaves

- 2 Tbsp freshly grated Parmesan cheese

Instructions:

1. Place a soup pot over medium flame and heat the oil. Stir in the onion and celery and sauté until caramelized.

2. Stir in the oregano, garlic, thyme, and basil and cook until fragrant. Stir in the red wine, then bring to a boil and cook until liquid is reduced by half.

3. Add the tomato paste and tomatoes, then the stock and stir. Bring to a boil, then reduce to a simmer. Partially cover and cook for half an hour.

4. Meanwhile, spiralize the celery, carrot, and parsnip into ribbons. Add to the pot and cook for 2 minutes or until tender.

5. Stir in the beans, vinegar, salt, and pepper. Spiralize the zucchini, then add to the pot. Remove from heat and serve at once. Top each serving with basil and cheese.

Spicy Tomato Chicken Noodle Soup

Number of Servings: 3

Ingredients:

- 1 cup zucchini noodles

- 3 cups chicken broth

- 14 oz roasted tomatoes

- 2 boneless, skinless chicken breasts

- 3 garlic cloves, minced

- 1 small yellow onion, chopped

- 1/2 cup chopped fresh cilantro

- 1 small jalapeno pepper, seeded and minced

- 1 medium carrot, sliced

- Juice of 1 lime

- 1 Tbsp olive oil

- 1/2 tsp turmeric

- 1/2 tsp cumin

- 1/2 tsp black pepper

Instructions:

1. Place a soup pot over medium flame and heat the oil. Add the onion, garlic, and carrots and cook until onions become tender.

2. Stir in the roasted tomatoes with juices, chicken breasts, and broth. Increase heat to a boil, and stir until chicken is well done. Take the chicken out of the soup and place in a bowl; set aside.

3. Set heat to medium low and let it simmer, covered. Shred the chicken and add back into the soup, together with the zucchini noodles, turmeric, cumin, and black pepper.

4. Stir in the lime juice and simmer for 20 seconds. Ladle into soup bowls and serve at once.

Creamy Veggie Gazpacho

Number of Servings: 2

Ingredients:

- 1 medium Persian or English cucumber, spiralized into ribbons
- 1/2 white onion, spiralized into ribbons
- 1 small green tomato, chopped
- 1 garlic clove, minced
- 1/2 celery stalk, chopped
- 1/2 cup spinach leaves or watercress
- 1/2 cup fresh cilantro leaves
- 1/4 cup chopped toasted almonds
- 1/2 tsp ground cumin
- 1/4 tsp ground coriander
- 1/4 tsp sea salt
- 1/4 tsp freshly ground black pepper
- 1/2 avocado, pitted and diced
- 1/2 cup plain non fat Greek yogurt
- 1/2 green onion, minced
- Juice and grated zest of 1/2 lime

Instructions:

1. Reserve half each of the spiralized cucumber and onion.

2. In a blender, mix together half of the cucumber and onion, tomato, celery, and garlic. Pulse until chunky, then add the lime juice and zest, watercress, almonds, and cilantro. Puree the mixture, then add enough water to create a smooth consistency.

3. Add the salt, pepper, coriander,, and cumin. Process to combine, then add the avocado and yogurt. Pulse until smooth. Pour the mixture into a bowl, then chill for half an hour.

4. Divide the cucumber and onion ribbons between two bowls and add the chilled gazpacho over each serving. Top with chopped green onion and serve at once.

Southeast Asian Chicken Noodle Soup

Number of Servings: 2

Ingredients:

- 1/4 cup zucchini noodles

- 1 boneless, skinless chicken breast, chopped

- 2 1/2 cups chicken broth

- 1/2 cup coconut milk

- 1 jalapeno pepper, seeded and minced

- 1 large garlic clove, chopped

- 3/4 inch piece fresh ginger root, grated

- 1/2 Tbsp lime zest

- 2 Tbsp freshly squeezed lime juice

- 2 Tbsp fish sauce

- 1 cup sliced shiitake mushrooms

- 1 cup baby spinach leaves

- 1 Tbsp chopped cilantro

Instructions:

1. Place a saucepan over medium flame and add the chicken broth, garlic, jalapeno, ginger, and lime zest and juice. Stir as you bring to a simmer.

2. Stir in the zucchini noodles and cook for 45 seconds or until tender. Take the noodles out with a pair of tongs and transfer to a bowl.

3. Stir the mushrooms into the soup, then let simmer for 3 minutes before adding the coconut milk and chicken. Let simmer until chicken is well done.

4. Stir in the spinach and cook until wilted, then add the chopped cilantro.

5. Ladle the soup into bowls and add the zucchini noodles into each. Serve at once.

Chapter 5 - Snack and Side Dish Recipes

Sauteed Summer Squash Spaghetti

Number of Servings: 4

Ingredients:

- 1 lb summer squash, spiralized into ribbons

- 1/2 lb ripe Roma tomatoes, sliced thinly

- 1 small yellow onion, sliced thinly

- 1 1/2 Tbsp olive oil

- 1 large garlic clove, minced

- 1/4 tsp crushed dried red pepper flakes

- 1/2 Tbsp Italian seasoning

- Parmesan cheese

Instructions:

1. Place a skillet over medium flame and heat the olive oil. Add the onion and garlic and sauté until tender and fragrant.

2. Stir in the tomatoes until tender, then add the squash and gently sauté for 1 minute.

3. Season with the Italian seasoning and red pepper flakes, then toss to coat. Transfer to a plate and top with Parmesan cheese. Serve at once.

Potato and Spinach Casserole

Number of Servings: 3

Ingredients:

- 2 cups baking potato ribbons, blanched

- 1 cup sliced mushrooms

- 2 cups chicken broth

- 1 small yellow onion, chopped

- 1 garlic clove, minced

- 5 oz frozen chopped spinach, thawed and squeezed dry

- 1 1/4 cups milk, dairy or nut

- 1/2 Tbsp olive oil

- 2 Tbsp grated Parmesan or feta cheese

- 1/4 tsp black pepper

Instructions:

1. Set the oven to 350 degrees F to preheat. Lightly grease a small baking dish with nonstick cooking spray, oil, or butter.

2. Place a skillet over medium flame and heat the olive oil. Stir in the onion, garlic, and mushrooms, and cook until onions become translucent.

3. Stir the broth and black pepper into the skillet. Increase to medium high heat and continue to stir until broth is almost completely evaporated.

4. Add the spinach and cook until wilted.

5. Place half the potato ribbons into the baking dish and scrape half of the spinach mixture over them. Repeat.

6. In a bowl, whisk the eggs, milk, and cornstarch together, then pour on top of the potato and spinach mixture evenly.

7. Bake for 30 to 45 minutes, then sprinkle the cheese on top and bake for an additional 10 minutes, or until the top is brown and bubbly.

8. Set on a wire rack to cool for at least 3 minutes before serving.

Shrimp Ceviche with Cucumber and Jicama

Number of Servings: 2

Ingredients:

- 1/2 lb medium shrimp, shelled, deveined, and chopped
- 1 small Persian or English cucumber, spiralized into shreds
- Juice and grated zest of 1 1/2 limes
- Juice and grated zest of 1/2 orange
- 1/2 small Jicama, spiralized into shreds
- 1 jalapeno pepper, seeded and minced
- 1/2 red bell pepper, diced
- 1 small tomato, diced
- 1/2 cup fresh cilantro leaves
- 1 Tbsp olive oil
- 1/2 tsp ground cumin
- 1/4 tsp ground coriander
- 1/2 tsp sea salt
- 1/4 tsp freshly ground black pepper
- 1 small ripe avocado, diced

Instructions:

1. Combine the lime juice and zest and chopped shrimp in a bowl. Refrigerate for 1 hour.

2. Place the shredded cucumber and Jicama in a bowl and add cold water, then refrigerate.

3. Place the minced jalapeno in a bowl, then stir in the diced bell pepper, cilantro, and tomato. Mix in the orange juice and zest, salt, pepper, coriander, and cumin. Toss to coat.

4. Place a nonstick skillet over medium flame and coat with nonstick cooking spray. Add the shrimp and cook until pink and firm, then scrape into the cilantro mixture.

5. Add the Jicama and cucumber shreds into the mixture and toss well to coat. Adjust seasoning, if necessary.

6. Before serving, toss in the avocado.

Vegetable and Rosemary Sides

Number of Servings: 4

Ingredients:

- 1 1/2 cups carrot ribbons, raw or blanched

- 1 cup turnip ribbons, raw or blanched

- 1 1/2 cups yellow squash ribbons, raw or blanched

- 1 cup julienned sweet potato, blanched

- 1 bell pepper, seeded and julienned

- 1 small yellow onion, sliced thinly

- 1/2 bunch fresh rosemary, chopped

- 2 fresh sage leaves, chopped (or 1/2 tsp dried)

- 1/2 Tbsp Italian seasoning

- 1 1/2 Tbsp balsamic vinegar

- 2 garlic cloves, minced

- 1/2 tsp black pepper

- 1 1/2 Tbsp olive oil

Instructions:

1. In a jar, combine the rosemary, sage, Italian seasoning, balsamic vinegar, garlic, and black pepper. Seal and shake vigorously to combine.

2. Place a skillet over medium flame and heat the olive oil. Add the sweet potato, bell pepper, and onion and sauté until almost tender.

3. Reduce heat and toss in the carrot, turnip, and yellow squash ribbons. Carefully sauté until tender.

4. Drizzle the balsamic vinegar mixture over the contents in the skillet and carefully toss to coat. Cook for 1 minute or until fragrant, then transfer to a dish and serve.

Sweet Potato Shoestring Fries

Number of Servings: 4

Ingredients:

- 4 Tbsp olive oil

- 2 large sweet potatoes

- Sea salt

- Freshly ground black pepper

- Optional: cayenne pepper

Instructions:

1. Set the oven to 400 degrees F to preheat.

2. Slice the ends off the sweet potatoes, then spiralize them into long shreds. Toss the shreds in olive oil. Season with salt, pepper, and cayenne, if using.

3. Line a baking sheet with parchment paper and arrange the potato shreds on it. Bake for 25 minutes, then serve.

Spicy Cabbage and Carrot Noodles

Number of Servings: 3

Ingredients:

- 2 cups spiralized green cabbage, raw or blanched
- 1 1/2 cups carrot ribbons, raw or blanched
- 1 1/2 Tbsp apple cider vinegar
- 1 1/2 Tbsp olive oil
- 1/2 Tbsp brown sugar or granulated sugar substitute
- 1/4 tsp dry mustard
- 1/8 tsp pepper
- 1/4 tsp hot pepper sauce

Instructions:

1. In a bowl, toss together the cabbage and carrot noodles.

2. In a bowl, whisk together the vinegar, olive oil, sugar, dry mustard, pepper, and hot pepper sauce. Drizzle the mixture on top of the vegetables.

3. Toss carefully to coat, then cover the bowl and refrigerate for 1 to 3 hours to intensify the flavors. Serve chilled.

Crunchy Garlic Potato Fries

Number of Servings: 3

Ingredients:

- 1 large russet potato
- 1/2 garlic bulb, peeled and minced
- 1 Tbsp olive oil
- 1 tsp garlic salt
- 1 tsp freshly ground black pepper

Instructions:

1. Set the oven to 400 degrees F to preheat.

2. Spiralize the potatoes into long, thin shreds. Drizzle olive oil over the potato shreds and toss to coat. Season with pepper and garlic salt. Toss together with the minced garlic.

3. Line a baking sheet using parchment paper, then place the potato shreds on it.

4. Bake for 30 minutes, or until crisp. Serve at once.

Mexican Slaw

Number of Servings: 3

Ingredients:

- 1 cup spiralized green cabbage

- 1 cup spiralized Napa cabbage

- 1 cup red radishes, trimmed and sliced thinly

- 1 fresh poblano or Hatch chili, seeded and diced

- Juice of 1 1/2 limes

- 1/2 Tbsp canola oil

- 1 cup minced fresh cilantro

- 1/8 tsp cayenne pepper

Instructions:

1. In a bowl, toss together the cabbages, radishes, and chili.

2. In a bowl, mix the lime juice and cayenne pepper well. Stir in the cilantro, then set aside for 5 minutes to let the flavors meld. Stir in the oil.

3. Drizzle the dressing all over the cabbage mixture and toss to coat. Chill for at least 1 hour or serve at once.

Parsnip Chips with Special Herb Dip

Number of Servings: 6

Ingredients:

- 2 anchovy fillets
- 2 garlic cloves
- 1 1/2 cups mayonnaise
- 2/3 cup fresh flat leaf parsley leaves
- 1/3 cup fresh mint or tarragon leaves
- 3 green onions
- Juice and grated zest of 1 1/2 lemons
- 2/3 tsp sea salt, plus more to taste
- 2/3 tsp freshly ground black pepper
- 6 large parsnips
- 3 Tbsp olive oil

Instructions:

1. In a blender, combine the garlic, anchovy, parsley, tarragon, green onion, mayonnaise, 2/3 teaspoon salt, pepper, and mayonnaise. Blend until smooth, then transfer to a bowl, cover, and refrigerate.

2. Set the oven to 375 degrees F to preheat. Line a baking sheet with parchment paper.

3. Spiralize the parsnip into spiral ribbons, then coat with the olive oil. Arrange on the prepared baking sheet and bake for 12 minutes, or until crisp, stirring occasionally.

4. Season with salt, then set on a wire rack to cool. Serve with the chilled dip.

Creamy Artichoke Slaw

Number of Servings: 3

Ingredients:

- 1 small carrot, julienned
- 1/4 lb Jerusalem artichokes, peeled and julienned
- 1 Tbsp Greek yogurt
- 1 Tbsp sour cream
- 1/2 tsp dry mustard
- 1 tsp white wine vinegar
- 1/8 tsp black pepper
- 1/2 Tbsp chopped fresh parsley

Instructions:

1. In a bowl, stir together the sour cream, Greek yogurt, vinegar, and mustard. Stir in the black pepper and adjust seasoning to taste.

2. In a bowl, combine the carrot and artichokes, then pour the sour cream mixture on top. Carefully toss to coat.

3. Cover the bowl and chill for at least 1 hour to let the flavors combine well. Serve chilled.

Chapter 6 - Sweet Recipes

Apple and Cinnamon Pancakes

Number of Servings: 3

Ingredients:

- 1 cup almond flour

- 1 tsp baking powder

- 1/4 cup brown sugar or stevia

- 1/2 tsp salt

- 1/4 tsp cinnamon

- 1 large egg

- 1/3 cup milk

- 1/2 tsp vanilla extract

- 2 apples, cored and spiralized

- 2 Tbsp coconut oil

Instructions:

1. Combine the baking powder, salt, flour, cinnamon, and sugar or stevia in a bowl.

2. In another bowl, beat the egg, then add the vanilla and milk. Pour the mixture into the dry

ingredients and mix until combined; do not over-mix.

3. Stir the thin apple ribbons into the batter, then set aside for 8 minutes at room temperature.

4. Place a nonstick skillet over medium flame and heat the oil until simmering. Ladle some of the batter into the skillet and cook until bubbly, then flip over and cook until golden brown.

5. Transfer the pancake to a plate lined with paper towels, then repeat with the remaining batter. Serve at once with raw honey or maple syrup.

Fried Apple Cinnamon Ribbons

Number of Servings: 2

Ingredients:

- 2 cups unpeeled apples, cored and spiralized into ribbons
- 2 1/2 Tbsp brown sugar or granulated sugar substitute
- 1/4 cup coconut oil
- 1 1/4 Tbsp cinnamon

Instructions:

1. In a small bowl, combine the cinnamon and sugar.

2. Place a skillet over medium flame and melt the coconut oil.

3. Carefully lay the apple ribbons onto the hot skillet and sprinkle the cinnamon and sugar mixture on both sides.

4. Cook until tender, then transfer to a plate lined with paper towels. Drain, then serve.

Minty Pear and Pomegranate Salad

Number of Servings: 2

Ingredients:

- 1/2 Tbsp brown sugar or stevia

- 1/2 tsp orange flower water

- Juice and zest of 1/2 orange

- 2 Asian pears, spiralized into ribbons

- 1/4 cup pomegranate seeds (or 1/2 cup fresh blueberries)

- 2 Tbsp minced fresh mint leaves

- 2 gingersnap cookies, crushed

- Sea salt

Instructions:

1. Place a saucepan over medium flame and add 1/2 tablespoon of water, stir in the brown sugar and bring to a boil.

2. Once boiling, immediately remove from heat and stir in the orange zest and juice, a dash of salt, and orange flower water. Set aside.

3. In a bowl, gently toss together the pear ribbons, mint, and pomegranate seeds. Drizzle the cooled syrup on top and gently toss to coat.

Cover the bowl and chill for about 30 minutes to 1 hour.

4. Before serving, top with crushed gingersnap cookies.

Rhubarb and Apple Compote

Number of Servings: 3

Ingredients:

- 2 rhubarb stalks, diced
- 3 Red Delicious apples, peeled, cored, and spiralized into ribbons
- 1/4 cup brown sugar or granulated sugar substitute
- 1/2 Tbsp vanilla extract
- 1 Tbsp unsalted butter
- 1/8 tsp cinnamon
- 1/8 tsp ground ginger

Instructions:

1. In a saucepan, melt the butter over medium flame. Stir in the vanilla extract and sugar until sugar melts.

2. Add the diced rhubarb and apple ribbons into the saucepan. Let it simmer for 20 minutes or until fruit becomes extra tender and sauce becomes thick.

3. Serve warm, at room temperature, or chilled.

Carrot Cupcakes

Number of Servings: 6 cupcakes

Ingredients:

- 2 large carrots, spiralized
- 1 cup brown sugar
- 3/4 cup coconut oil, melted and cooled
- 2 eggs
- 1 cup almond flour
- 1 tsp baking powder
- 3/4 tsp baking soda
- 1/2 tsp sea salt
- 1/2 tsp cinnamon
- 1 tsp ground nutmeg
- 1/2 tsp cardamom

Instructions:

1. Set the oven to 375 degrees F to preheat. Line 6 muffin tins with paper liners.

2. In a bowl, beat the eggs together with the oil and sugar. Sift in the baking soda, salt, flour, and spices. Mix until combined.

3. Fold the spiralized carrots into the batter, then divide among the muffin tins.

4. Bake for 15 minutes, or until puffed and firm at the center. Set on a wire rack to cool for 5 minutes, then serve.

Carrot and Coconut Pudding

Number of Servings: 3

Ingredients:

- 1/4 cup dark raisins

- 1/4 cup golden raisins

- 2 Tbsp currants

- 2 Tbsp chopped pitted dates

- 2 medium carrots, spiralized into shreds

- 1 Tbsp brandy or dark rum

- 1 egg

- 2 Tbsp brown sugar or granulated sugar substitute

- 1/8 tsp ground cardamom

- 1/8 tsp ground nutmeg

- 1/8 tsp cinnamon

- 1/16 tsp ground clove

- 1/2 Tbsp vanilla extract

- 1 1/2 cups heavy cream, dairy or nut

- 1 cup cooked rice

- 1/2 cup shredded coconut

Instructions:

1. In a bowl, toss together the raisins, currants, and dates. Add 3/4 cup boiling water and the rum. Let stand for 1 to 12 hours.

2. Set the oven to 375 degrees F to preheat. Grease a baking dish with nonstick cooking spray.

3. In a bowl, beat the egg with the vanilla, spices, and sugar. Stir in the cream and mix well. Add the carrot, coconut, and rice. Mix well.

4. Drain the soaked dried fruit and fold into the mixture. Pour the mixture into the prepared baking dish.

5. Bake for 25 to 30 minutes or until pudding is set and golden brown.

6. Chill and serve cool or serve at once, preferably with cinnamon or whipped cream.

Carrot Candy Strings

Number of Servings: 12 servings

Ingredients:

- 1 large carrot, spiralized into strings

- 1/2 cup granulated sugar

Instructions:

1. Boil 1 1/2 cups of water in a saucepan, then add the spiralized carrots. Cook for 1 minute, then strain and set aside.

2. Stir the sugar into 1/2 cup of water, then boil in a saucepan. Add the carrot, then reduce the flame and let simmer for 5 minutes.

3. Drain the syrup and arrange the carrot strings on a sheet of parchment paper to dry. Transfer into a tightly sealed container and freeze.

Peach Ice Cream

Number of Servings: 3

Ingredients:

- 2 peaches or nectarines, pitted and halved

- 1/2 Tbsp brown sugar or granulated sugar substitute

- 1/4 tsp vanilla extract

- 1/2 pint vanilla ice cream

- 1/2 pint fresh raspberries

Instructions:

1. Spiralize the peaches or nectarines to create spiral ribbons. Place in a bowl.

2. Add the vanilla and sugar into the bowl and toss the peach or nectarine ribbons to coat. Set aside for at least 6 minutes.

3. Divide the peach or nectarine mixture into three servings and add a scoop of ice cream on top of each. Sprinkle the raspberries on top, then serve at once.

Honey and Melon Compote

Number of Servings: 2

Ingredients:

- 1 1/2 Tbsp honey
- 1/2 inch fresh ginger root, peeled and grated
- Juice and grated zest of 1/2 orange
- 1 medium cantaloupe or honeydew melon
- 1/4 tsp freshly ground pink peppercorns
- 1/4 tsp freshly ground black pepper
- 3 fresh mint leaves, minced

Instructions:

1. Place a saucepan over medium flame and add the honey and ginger. Stir in the orange juice and zest and let simmer until thoroughly combined. Remove from heat and set aside to cool to room temperature.

2. Slice the ends of the melon, then slice off the skin. Slice into the appropriate size and spiralize into strings or flat ribbons. Place in a bowl.

3. Add the honey mixture on top of the melon, then add the mint and peppercorns. Toss carefully to coat.

4. Serve at once, preferably with yogurt or ice cream.

Sweet Potato Pie

Number of Servings: 4

Ingredients:

- 1 1/2 cups and 1/2 tsp almond flour
- 1/2 tsp sea salt
- 1/2 Tbsp brown sugar or granulated sugar substitute
- 4 oz chilled unsalted butter
- 1/4 cup ice water
- 1/2 tsp cider vinegar
- 2 large sweet potatoes, spiralized into thin ribbons
- 1/2 tsp nutmeg
- 1 Tbsp brown sugar
- 1/4 tsp cinnamon
- 1/8 tsp sea salt
- 1 egg

Instructions:

1. In a bowl, mix together the 1 1/2 cups of flour, 1/2 tablespoon of brown sugar, and 1/2

teaspoon of salt. Slice the butter into the mixture until you create a coarse mixture.

2. Gradually add the water, stirring with a fork, until you have a dough. Wrap the dough in plastic wrap and chill for 2 hours or more.

3. Boil water in a pot. Add the spiralized sweet potatoes and cook for 1 to 2 minutes, or until softened. Drain well, then place in a bowl.

4. Add the remaining brown sugar and flour into the bowl, followed by the nutmeg, cinnamon, and 1/2 teaspoon sea salt. Toss carefully to coat the sweet potatoes.

5. Grease a 5 inch pie pan or 4 small pie tins with nonstick cooking spray. Knead three fourths of the dough well and flatten into a 1/4 inch thick layer with a rolling pin.

6. Line the pan with the dough, then add the sweet potato mixture in. Add some more butter on top of each. Roll out the remaining dough and cut it into strips to make your pie crust.

7. Layer the strips of dough on top of the pie and crimp the edges. Place the pie in the freezer for half an hour.

8. Set the oven to 350 degrees F to preheat.

9. In a bowl, beat the egg with 1/2 tablespoon of water and brush it on top of the pie. Top with a bit of sugar, then bake for 20 minutes, or until golden brown.

10. Set oven to 325 degrees F and keep baking for 10 minutes or until bubbly.

11. Take the pie out of the oven and set on a wire rack to cool. Slice, then serve, preferably with whipped cream or ice cream.

Chapter 7 - Breakfast

Baked Apple Pancake

Makes: 2 servings

Ingredients:

- 1 apple, stemmed and cored
- 3 Tbsp coconut oil, melted
- 1/8 tsp ground nutmeg
- 1 tsp ground cinnamon
- 1/4 cup coconut milk
- 2 small eggs
- 1/2 tsp vanilla extract
- 1/8 tsp baking soda
- 1/8 tsp stevia
- 1 Tbsp coconut flour
- Sea salt

Instructions:

1. Set the oven to 425 degrees F to preheat.

2. Slice the ends off the apple and spiralize into ribbon noodles. Slice the ribbon noodles crosswise and set aside.

3. Place an ovenproof frying pan over medium high flame and heat 1 tablespoon of coconut oil. Add the cinnamon and nutmeg into the oil, then put the apple ribbon noodles into the pan in a single layer. Cook for 5 minutes, or until browned. Do not stir.

4. While waiting for the apple ribbons to cook, mix together the rest of the melted coconut oil with the coconut milk, stevia, coconut flour, vanilla extract, eggs, baking soda, and a dash of salt in a blender. Set the blender on high speed and mix the ingredients until thoroughly combined.

5. Pour the batter on top of the apples in the frying pan. Take the pan off the heat and place it in the preheated oven.

6. Bake for 10 minutes, or until the pancake is puffy.

7. Slice and serve at once.

Pear and Sweet Potato Pudding

Makes: 2 servings

Ingredients:

- 1 small sweet potato, peeled
- 1 small pear, peeled and cored
- 1 Tbsp. coconut oil
- 1/4 cup coconut milk
- 1/8 tsp ground nutmeg
- 1/4 tsp ground cinnamon
- Sea salt

Instructions:

1. Slice the ends off the sweet potato, then spiralize it into spaghetti noodles. Place the sweet potato noodles into a food processor and pulse for a second about 20 times until it becomes grainy.

2. Dice the pear into 1/4 inch cubes.

3. Heat the coconut oil over medium high flame in a medium skillet until shimmery.

4. Gently stir the diced pear in the coconut oil for about 5 minutes, or until partially browned.

5. Add the sweet potato *rice* into the skillet and stir gently for an additional 3 minutes, or until browned and tender.

6. Add the coconut milk, nutmeg, cinnamon, and a dash of salt. Stir everything together for about 3 minutes, or until the flavors meld.

7. Pour into two bowls and serve at once.

Parsnip Waffles

Makes: 4 servings

Ingredients:

- 4 large parsnips, peeled

- 1 Tbsp olive oil

- 1/2 tsp garlic powder

- 2 large eggs

- 6 Tbsp chopped fresh chives

- 4 tsp lemon juice

- Sea salt

- Freshly ground black pepper

Instructions:

1. Turn on the Belgian waffle iron to preheat.

2. Slice the ends off the parsnips and spiralize them into spaghetti noodles. Slice the noodles into half inch bits.

3. Place a frying pan over medium flame and heat the olive oil. Stir in the parsnip noodles and add a dash of salt and pepper. Add the garlic powder and toss gently to coat.

4. Cover the pan and cook for about 5 minutes or until the noodles are tender. Turn off the heat and set aside to cool down slightly.

5. Meanwhile, beat the eggs in a bowl together with the chives. Fold in the parsnip noodles and mix well.

6. Coat the waffle iron using nonstick cooking spray, then fill it with half of the parsnip noodle mixture. Cook based on manufacturer's settings, then remove and place on a platter. Repeat with the second batch.

7. Serve the waffles warm, preferably with Paleo-friendly yogurt, high quality maple syrup, or with crispy bacon.

Cabbage and Apple Hash with Egg

Makes: 4 serving

Ingredients:

- 2 apples, stemmed and cored

- 4 Tbsp coconut oil

- 1 red onion, minced

- 1/2 medium red cabbage, cored, outer leaves discarded

- 4 eggs

- 2 tsp dried thyme

- 2 garlic cloves, minced

- 2 Tbsp red wine vinegar

- 1 tsp sea salt

- 1/2 tsp freshly ground black pepper

Instructions:

1. Slice the ends off the apples, then spiralize them into spaghetti noodles. Slice into half inch bits and set aside.

2. If you have an hourglass spiralizer, spiralize the cabbage into spaghetti noodles as well. Otherwise, simply chop them roughly.

3. Fill a pot halfway with water and stir in the red wine vinegar. Place over medium low heat.

4. Place a frying pan over medium high flame, then heat the coconut oil until shimmery. Add the apple noodles, cabbage, and red onion. Season with the salt, pepper, and dried thyme.

5. Stir gently as you cook for about 10 minutes, or until the mixture is partially browned. Stir in the garlic and cook for half a minute, or until fragrant.

6. Meanwhile, once the water in the pot is simmering, crack one egg into a bowl and then carefully slip it into the simmering water. Repeat with the remaining eggs. Cook for 4 minutes to poach.

7. Distribute the cabbage and apple hash among four plates. Then, using a slotted spoon, take a poached egg out of the pot and place it on top of the heap of hash. Repeat until you have 4 servings. Serve at once.

Plantain and Coconut Pudding

Makes: 2 servings

Ingredients:

- 2 plantain, medium ripe, peeled

- 1/4 tsp cinnamon

- 3 tsp coconut flakes

- 1/2 cup raisins

- 2 1/2 cups vanilla almond milk

Instructions:

1. Slice the ends off the plantain and spiralize them into spaghetti noodles. Place the plantain noodles into the food processor and pulse until grainy.

2. Place the plantain grains into a saucepan and stir in about 2 cups of almond milk. Place over medium high flame and bring to a boil, then reduce to a simmer.

3. Let the mixture simmer for about 5 minutes, then gradually pour in the remaining almond milk and let simmer to a desired consistency.

4. Turn off the heat and stir in the coconut flakes, raisins, and cinnamon. Divide between two bowls and serve.

Zucchini and Onion Biscuits with Special Gravy

Makes: 6 servings

Ingredients:

- 2 small zucchinis
- 1 small onion, minced
- 3/4 cup almond meal flour
- 1 1/2 Tbsp heavy coconut cream
- 3/4 tsp baking powder
- 1 1/2 Tbsp sea salt
- 2 small eggs
- 1/3 tsp freshly ground black pepper

For the Special Gravy

- 3 cups meat or chicken stock
- 3 oz dried porcini mushrooms
- 12 oz bulk breakfast sausage
- 3 Tbsp coconut oil or ghee
- 1 small onion, minced
- 12 oz sliced button mushrooms
- 1 1/2 tsp dried thyme
- 1/3 cup arrowroot powder

- 1/3 cup water

- 2 tsp sea salt

- 1/3 tsp freshly ground black pepper

- 3 Tbsp heavy coconut cream

Instructions:

1. In the previous night, combine the stock and porcini mushrooms in a bowl. Cover the bowl using plastic wrap, then refrigerate for at least 8 hours to soak.

2. The following morning, slice the ends off the zucchini, then spiralize them into spaghetti noodles. Place them in a colander and season with about 1 1/2 tablespoons of salt. Set aside for half an hour.

3. Take the mushrooms out of the stock; do not discard the stock. Press as much stock out of the mushrooms, then mince and set aside.

4. Place a large frying pan over medium high flame and melt the coconut oil or ghee. Cook the breakfast sausage and crumble it up using a wooden spoon. Continue to cook for 6 minutes, or until browned. Transfer to a platter and set aside.

5. Sauté the onion, chopped porcini mushrooms, and button mushrooms in the same pan. Add the thyme and sauté carefully for 5 minutes, or until browned.

6. Stir the saved stock into the frying pan and let the mixture simmer.

7. Meanwhile, combine the arrowroot powder, salt, pepper, and water very well. Pour the mixture into the frying pan and stir to combine. Cook until thickened.

8. Add the coconut cream and stir to combine. Turn off the heat, cover, and set aside.

9. To make the biscuits, set the oven first at 400 degrees F to preheat. Cover a baking sheet using parchment paper.

10. Rinse the zucchini noodles and blot dry using paper towels. Place the zucchini noodles in a bowl and mix it with the onion, baking powder, almond meal flour, coconut cream, eggs, pepper, and remaining salt.

11. Using a tablespoon drop the biscuits on the baking sheet. Bake for 10 minutes, or until golden brown. Flip the biscuits over with a spatula and bake for an additional 10 minutes. Remove from the oven and set on a wire rack to cool slightly.

12. Reheat the gravy before serving. Arrange the biscuits on a platter and spoon the gravy on top. Serve warm.

Butternut Squash Waffles

Makes: 8 servings

Ingredients:

- 1/2 medium butternut squash, peeled
- 1 1/2 cups almond flour
- 4 tsp baking powder
- 1 cup arrowroot powder
- 2 tsp ground cinnamon
- 4 Tbsp coconut oil, melted
- 1 tsp stevia
- 2 1/2 cups coconut milk
- Sea salt

Instructions:

1. Turn on the Belgian waffle iron to preheat.

2. Slice the ends off the butternut squash and spiralize them into spaghetti noodles. Slice the noodles into half inch bits.

3. In a bowl, combine the almond flour, baking powder, stevia, arrowroot powder, cinnamon, and a pinch of salt.

4. In a separate bowl, combine 2 tablespoons of coconut oil with the coconut milk.

5. Create a pit in the center of the almond flour mixture and pour into it the coconut milk mixture. Let the dry ingredients collapse into the wet ingredients, then mix everything until just combined; do not over-mix.

6. Gently mix in the butternut squash noodles.

7. Coat the waffle iron using the remaining coconut oil, then fill it with a quarter of the batter. Cook based on manufacturer's settings, then remove the waffles and place on a platter. Repeat with the remaining batter.

8. Serve the waffles warm, preferably with high quality maple syrup. Freeze leftover waffles and reheat in the waffle iron within 2 days.

Sweet Potato Hash Browns with Special Salsa

Makes: 4 servings

Ingredients:

- 2 sweet potatoes, peeled
- 1 avocado
- 8 scallions, white and green parts, sliced thinly
- 2 ancho chilies, seeded and minced
- 1/2 cup olive oil, divided
- 2 tsp chili powder
- 1 tsp sea salt
- 1 tsp ground cumin
- 2 tsp chili powder
- 1/2 tsp freshly ground black pepper

For the Salsa:

- 1 medium tomato, seeded and minced
- 2 jalapeno peppers, seeded and minced
- 1 red onion, mined
- 4 Tbsp chopped fresh cilantro
- Juice of 1 lime

- 1/2 tsp sea salt

Instructions:

1. Slice the ends off the sweet potatoes, then spiralize them into spaghetti noodles. Slice the noodles into half inch bits and place in a large bowl.

2. Add the scallions, ancho chilies, cumin, chili powder, salt, pepper, and 4 tablespoons of the olive oil to the sweet potato noodles. Mix well.

3. Place a large frying pan over medium high flame and heat the remaining olive oil. Pour the sweet potato mixture into the pan and spread it out to create an even layer. Cook for 5 minutes or until browned; do not stir.

4. With a spatula, flip the hash brown over and cook for an additional 5 minutes.

5. Meanwhile, combine all of the ingredients for the salsa in a bowl. Slice the avocado in half lengthwise, then remove the core. Spoon the flesh out and dice.

6. Place the hash brown on a platter and spoon the salsa and avocado on top. Slice into wedges and serve at once.

Nutty Carrot Pancakes

Makes: 2 servings

Ingredients:

- 1 carrot, peeled
- 1/3 cup almond flour
- 1/8 tsp stevia
- 2 Tbsp arrowroot powder
- 3/4 tsp baking powder
- 1/4 tsp ground cinnamon
- 1/8 tsp ground ginger
- 1/2 cup coconut milk
- 1 Tbsp coconut oil, melted
- 1/2 tsp vanilla extract
- 2 Tbsp minced walnuts

Instructions:

1. Slice the ends off the carrot and spiralize into spaghetti noodles. Slice the noodles into half inch bits and set aside.

2. Combine the almond flour, stevia, arrowroot powder, salt, baking powder, cinnamon, and ginger in a bowl.

3. In another bowl, add the coconut milk and vanilla extract. Stir in half of the melted coconut oil.

4. Create a small well in the center of the almond flour mixture, then slowly pour the coconut milk mixture into it. Let the dry ingredients collapse into the wet ingredients, then stir until combined. Be careful not to over-mix.

5. Add the walnuts and carrot noodles, mixing gently until evenly distributed in the batter.

6. Place a nonstick frying pan over medium high flame. Coat the base with the second half of the coconut oil.

7. Using a ladle, pour some of the batter into the skillet to make a pancake. Cook one side for about 2 minutes, then flip over and cook for an additional 1 or 2 minutes.

8. Stack the pancakes on a platter and serve with raw honey or high quality maple syrup.

Chapter 8 - Soups

Oriental Hot Chicken Noodle Soup

Makes: 2 servings

Ingredients:

- 9 oz skinless chicken breast

- 1 medium turnip, peeled

- 3 cups chicken stock

- 1 cup water

- 1/2 red bell pepper, sliced thinly

- 3 scallions, sliced thinly

- 1 tsp red curry paste

- 1/2 lime, sliced into wedges

- 2 Tbsp chopped fresh cilantro

Instructions:

1. Simmer the chicken, broth, and water in a pot over medium flame.

2. Reduce to low flame, cover and let simmer for 20 minutes or until the chicken is completely cooked.

3. Slice the ends off the turnip and spiralize into spaghetti noodles. Trim and set aside.

4. Turn off the heat under the pot, then take the chicken out of the pot and set aside. Once completely cooled, shred the meat off the bones and return the bones into the pot.

5. Bring soup to a boil, then cook for 10 minutes, uncovered, until mixture boils down to a third of its original volume.

6. Remove the bones with a slotted spoon from the pot. Stir the curry paste into the pot, then set to medium high flame and simmer.

7. Stir in the bell pepper and turnip noodles. Cook for 3 minutes, or until turnip noodles are al dente.

8. Add the scallions and shredded chicken meat into the pot. Stir to combine and cook for 1 minute.

9. Ladle into soup bowls and top with chopped fresh cilantro. Garnish with lime wedges and serve at once.

Mediterranean Jicama, Egg and Lemon Broth Soup

Makes: 2 servings

Ingredients:

- 1 small jicama, peeled

- 6 oz cooked chicken, chopped

- 3 cups meat or chicken stock

- 1/4 tsp sea salt

- 1/8 tsp freshly ground black pepper

- 1/4 cup freshly squeezed lemon juice

- 1 egg

Instructions:

1. Slice the ends off the jicama and spiralize into spaghetti noodles. Transfer to the food processor and pulse until it is grainy.

2. Transfer the jicama *rice* into a pot and stir in the stock, salt, and pepper. Place over medium high flame and let simmer for 5 minutes, or until the jicama *rice* is al dente.

3. Stir in the cooked chicken and let it simmer for 2 minutes.

4. Meanwhile, whisk the egg and lemon juice together. Slowly pour the mixture into the soup as you stir. Serve at once.

Really Red Gazpacho

Makes: 2 servings

Ingredients:

- 1 medium tomato, pureed
- 2 cups diced seedless watermelon
- 1/4 medium cucumber, diced
- 1 Tbsp minced red onion
- 2 Tbsp chopped fresh parsley
- 2 Tbsp chopped fresh dill, mint, or basil
- 1/2 Tbsp extra virgin olive oil
- 1/4 jalapeno, diced
- 1 medium beet, peeled
- Sea salt
- Freshly ground black pepper

Instructions:

1. Combine the tomato, watermelon, cucumber, onion, parsley, dill or mint or basil, and jalapeno in a food processor. Pulse as you gradually pour in the olive oil in a thin stream. Season to taste with salt and pepper.

2. Once a desired consistency is reached, transfer the mixture into a bowl, cover, and refrigerate until very chilled.

3. Slice the ends off the beet and spiralize into flat noodles.

4. To serve, pour the soup into bowls and top with the beet noodles. Always serve chilled.

Beef Noodle Soup

Makes: 2 servings

Ingredients:

- 1 Tbsp coconut oil

- 1 carrot, peeled and sliced thinly

- 2 scallions, white and green parts, sliced thinly

- 2 zucchinis

- 3 garlic cloves, sliced thinly

- 1/2 lb flank steak, sliced into 1/4 inch thick strips against the grain

- 1 celery stalk, sliced thinly

- 3 cups beef or chicken stock

- 1/2 Tbsp fish sauce

- 1/4 tsp Sriracha

- 1/4 tsp ground cinnamon

- 1/4 tsp freshly ground black pepper

- 1 1/2 Tbsp chopped fresh cilantro

Instructions:

1. Place a pot over medium high flame and heat the coconut oil.

2. Stir in the beef and cook for 6 minutes, or until browned. Use a pair of tongs or a slotted spoon to transfer the beef to a platter.

3. In the same pot, stir in the celery, carrot, and scallions. Cook for 3 minutes or until vegetables are tender, stirring occasionally.

4. Stir in the garlic and sauté for half a minute, then stir in the stock, cinnamon, pepper, sriracha, and fish sauce.

5. Slice the ends off the zucchini and spiralize into spaghetti noodles.

6. Bring soup to a simmer, then add the zucchini noodles and cook for 3 minutes, or until al dente.

7. Place the cooked beef back into the soup and let it simmer for 1 minute or until heated through.

8. Stir in the cilantro, remove from heat, and serve at once.

Shrimp and Bok Choy Soup

Makes: 2 servings

Ingredients:

- 1 zucchini
- 3 cups chicken stock
- 3/4 cup clam juice or seafood stock
- 1 small bok choy, trimmed and sliced thinly
- 1 lb raw shrimp, shelled and deveined
- 2 green onions, sliced thinly
- 1 Tbsp grated fresh ginger
- 1/2 Tbsp crushed red pepper flakes
- 2 garlic cloves, minced
- 1 1/2 Tbsp coconut oil
- 3 oz sliced shiitake mushrooms

Instructions:

1. Place a pot over medium flame and heat the coconut oil. Stir in the mushrooms, bok choy, ginger, red pepper flakes, and garlic. Cook for 1 minute, then stir in the stock and clam juice. Cover and increase heat to a boil.

2. Once the soup is boiling, stir in the shrimp and green onions. Reduce heat to medium high and cook for an additional 2 minutes.

3. Meanwhile, slice the ends off the zucchini and spiralize into spaghetti noodles. Once the shrimp is completely cooked in the soup, add the noodles and turn off the heat.

4. Set aside for 5 minutes to make the noodles tender, then serve.

Ginger Mushroom Soup with Cucumber and Carrot Noodles

Makes: 2 servings

Ingredients:

- 1 Tbsp coconut oil

- 1/4 onion, minced

- 1/2 tsp grated fresh ginger

- 4 oz shiitake mushrooms

- 7 1/2 oz canned full fat coconut milk

- 2 garlic cloves, minced

- Juice of 1 lime

- 1 small cucumber

- 1 medium carrot, peeled

- 1 1/2 Tbsp chopped fresh cilantro

- 1/4 tsp sea salt

- 1/4 tsp Sriracha

Instructions:

1. Slice the ends off the cucumber and carrot, then spiralize them into spaghetti noodles. Set aside.

2. Remove the stems from the shiitake mushrooms, then slice the caps.

3. Heat the coconut oil in a pot over medium high flame. Stir in the mushrooms and onion and cook for 3 minutes, or until the mushrooms are tender.

4. Stir in the ginger and garlic and cook for half a minute, or until fragrant.

5. Add the coconut milk, vegetable stock, salt, Sriracha, and lime juice. Increase heat and let simmer.

6. Stir in the cucumber and carrot noodles and cook for about 5 minutes, or until al dente.

7. Add the cilantro and stir well, then remove from heat and serve at once.

Pumpkin Noodle Soup

Makes: 3 servings

Ingredients:

- 1/4 medium pumpkin
- 2 1/2 cups vegetable stock
- 1 Tbsp olive oil
- 1 cup pureed pumpkin
- 1 small yellow onion, diced
- 1/4 Tbsp raw honey
- 1/2 tsp cinnamon
- 1 Tbsp chopped fresh sage or 1 tsp dried
- 1/8 tsp ground ginger
- 1/8 tsp cayenne pepper
- Nutmeg

Instructions:

1. Slice the pumpkin into manageable pieces and spiralize into ribbon noodles.

2. Place a pot over medium flame and heat the oil. Stir in the onion and sauté until translucent. Stir in the cinnamon, sage, ginger, cayenne pepper, and a dash of nutmeg.

3. Stir in the pureed pumpkin and vegetable stock. Increase heat to a boil, then reduce to a simmer.

4. Stir in the raw honey until the honey completely dissolves.

5. Add the pumpkin noodles and simmer for 1 minute. Remove from heat and serve at once.

Sweet Potato Miso Soup

Makes: 2 servings

Ingredients:

- 1 Tbsp coconut oil

- 4 oz shiitake mushrooms

- 3 cups vegetable stock

- 3 scallions, white and green parts, sliced thinly

- 1 1/2 Tbsp miso paste, gluten free

- 1/2 cup chopped kale, no ribs

- 1 small sweet potato, peeled

- Crushed red pepper flakes

Instructions:

1. Remove the stems from the shiitake mushrooms, then slice the caps.

2. Heat the coconut oil in a pot over medium flame.

3. Stir in the mushrooms and scallions. Cook for 3 minutes or until mushrooms become tender, stirring occasionally.

4. Stir in the garlic and cook for half a minute, or until fragrant.

5. Stir in the vegetable stock and miso paste. Add a dash of red pepper flakes, then slowly bring to a boil.

6. Meanwhile, slice the ends off the sweet potato and spiralize into spaghetti noodles.

7. Stir the kale and sweet potato noodles into the soup, then reduce to a simmer and cook for 5 minutes or until the noodles are al dente. Serve at once.

Thai Coconut and Chicken Soup with Pickled Cucumber Noodles

Makes: 2 servings

Ingredients:

- 7 oz canned coconut milk
- 6 oz boneless, skinless chicken breast, cubed
- 2 cups chicken stock
- 2 1/2 inches peeled ginger, sliced thickly
- 1/2 cup sliced shiitake mushrooms
- Zest of 1/2 lemon
- 1/2 Tbsp fish sauce
- 1/2 tsp Sriracha
- 1 Tbsp chopped fresh cilantro

For the pickled cucumber noodles:

- 1 small cucumber
- 1/2 cup rice vinegar
- 1/2 cup water
- 1 1/2 tsp sea salt
- 1/4 tsp stevia

Instructions:

1. Make the cucumber noodles the previous night. Combine the water, vinegar, salt, and stevia in a saucepan and place over medium high flame. Bring to a simmer and cook until salt is thoroughly dissolved.

2. Slice the ends off the cucumber and spiralize into spaghetti noodles. Place in a bowl and pour the hot brine on top. Set aside, uncovered, for half an hour.

3. Take the cucumber noodles out of the brine and place in a tightly sealed container and refrigerate for at least 8 hours. Excess noodles can be refrigerated for up to 30 days.

4. Make the soup by stick, combining the coconut milk, lemon zest, and ginger in a pot. Place over medium high flame and bring to a simmer.

5. Stir in the fish sauce, sriracha, mushrooms, and chicken. Simmer for 10 minutes.

6. Take the ginger out and add the cilantro. Stir everything to combine.

7. Remove the soup from the heat and ladle into soup bowls. Top with pickled cucumber noodles and serve.

Chapter 9 - Main Course

Fiery Shrimp and Zucchini Pasta

Makes: 2 servings

Ingredients:

- 3 zucchini
- 3 1/2 Tbsp olive oil, divided
- 1/2 lb large shrimp, peeled and deveined
- 1 small onion, chopped
- 2 garlic cloves
- 1/2 tsp crushed red pepper flakes
- 1/4 tsp sea salt
- 1/2 cup dry white wine
- 7 oz canned diced tomatoes, undrained
- 1 1/2 Tbsp chopped fresh flat leaf parsley
- 1/4 tsp dried oregano
- 1/8 tsp freshly ground black pepper

Instructions:

1. Mix together the shrimp, salt, and red pepper flakes in a large bowl, then set aside for at least 10 minutes.

2. Slice the ends off the zucchini s and spiralize them into spaghetti noodles. Set aside.

3. Place a sauté pan over medium high flame and heat 1 tablespoon of olive oil. Add the shrimp and sauté for 4 minutes, or until pink and completely cooked. Using a slotted spoon, transfer the shrimp to a plate and cover with foil to keep warm.

4. Heat the remaining olive oil in the same pan and sauté the onion for about 3 minutes, or until translucent. Stir in the garlic and cook for half a minute, or until fragrant.

5. Pour the white wine into the pan and scrape the bottom to loosen any browned bits. Stir in the tomatoes with their juices, pepper, and oregano. Cook until liquid evaporates.

6. Add the parsley, zucchini noodles, and cooked shrimp into the pan with the sauce and cook for about 3 minutes. Remove from heat and serve at once.

Tuna Noodle Casserole

Makes: 2 servings

Ingredients:

- 2 zucchini
- 2 1/2 Tbsp coconut oil, melted
- 1/2 celery stalk, minced
- 4 oz cremini mushrooms, sliced
- 1 garlic clove, minced
- 1/2 onion, chopped
- 5 oz canned chunky tuna in water, drained
- 1/2 cup beef or chicken stock
- 1/2 tsp garlic powder
- 1/2 tsp dried thyme
- 1/2 tsp onion powder
- 1/4 tsp freshly ground black pepper
- 1/4 cup almond meal
- 1/3 cup heavy coconut cream
- Sea salt

Instructions:

1. Slice the ends off the zucchini, then spiralize into flat ribbon noodles. Slice the zucchini noodles into 2 inch bits and place in a colander.

2. Season the zucchini noodles with salt and set aside for at least half an hour.

3. Rinse the noodles and blot dry using paper towels. Set aside.

4. Set the oven to 400 degrees F to preheat.

5. Place a skillet over medium high flame and heat 1 1/2 tablespoons of coconut oil. Sauté the mushrooms, onion, and celery until onion becomes translucent.

6. Stir in the tuna and cook for about 4 minutes, then stir in the garlic and cook for half a minute, or until fragrant.

7. Stir in the onion and garlic powders, stock, 1/4 teaspoon salt, pepper, and thyme. Stir every now and then as you cook for about 4 minutes, or until the liquids are half the original volume.

8. Add the heavy coconut cream and stir for about 3 minutes or until thoroughly combined.

9. Stir in the zucchini noodles and turn off the heat.

10. Transfer the mixture into a small baking dish, then bake for 20 minutes.

11. Meanwhile, combine the remaining coconut oil with the almond meal in a bowl. Mix well.

12. Take the casserole out of the oven and top it with the almond meal mixture. Bake for an additional 3 minutes, then serve.

Carrot Paella

Makes: 2 servings

Ingredients:

- 3 carrots, peeled
- 1/2 onion, chopped
- 1 Tbsp olive oil
- 3 oz Paleo-friendly chorizo
- 2 garlic cloves, minced
- 3 oz shrimp, peeled and deveined
- 1/2 cup beef or chicken stock
- 1/4 tsp sea salt
- 1/8 tsp freshly ground black pepper
- 1 1/2 Tbsp chopped fresh flat leaf parsley
- saffron

Instructions:

1. Slice the ends off the carrots and spiralize them into spaghetti noodles. Transfer to a food processor and pulse until grainy, then set aside.

2. Heat the olive oil over medium high flame in a sauté pan, then stir in the chorizo and cook until browned. Transfer the chorizo to a plate using a slotted spoon and set aside.

3. Drain some of the grease from the pan, then sauté the onion until translucent. Add the garlic and sauté until fragrant.

4. Stir the carrot *rice*, chorizo, chicken stock, salt, pepper, a dash of saffron, and the shrimp into the pan. Sauté for about 5 minutes or until the shrimp is pink and cooked through.

5. Turn off the heat and stir in the parsley. Transfer to a platter then serve at once.

Pesto Spaghetti

Makes: 2 servings

Ingredients:

- 3 zucchini

- 1 1/2 Tbsp olive oil

- Sea salt

For the Pesto:

- 1 cup fresh basil

- 2 Tbsp pine nuts

- 1/4 cup Paleo-friendly nut cheese, Parmesan substitute

- 1/4 tsp sea salt

- 1/8 tsp freshly ground black pepper

- 1/4 cup extra virgin olive oil

- 2 garlic cloves

Instructions:

1. Slice the ends off the zucchini and spiralize into spaghetti noodles. Transfer to a colander and season with sea salt. Set aside for half an hour.

2. Place a nonstick skillet over medium high flame and heat the olive oil. Add the zucchini

noodles and cook for 5 minutes or until al dente. Transfer to a platter and set aside.

3. Make the pesto by combining the basil, pine nuts, nut cheese, sea salt, black pepper, olive oil, and garlic in a food processor. Pulse until thoroughly combined.

4. Spoon the pesto onto the zucchini noodles and toss everything to coat. Serve at once.

Halibut and Cucumber Curry

Makes: 2 servings

Ingredients:

- 1 1/2 Tbsp olive oil

- 3 cucumbers

- 1/4 onion, minced

- 1 tsp curry powder

- 1 cup beef or poultry stock

- 1/4 cup coconut milk

- 2 skinless halibut fillets, 4 oz each

- 2 Tbsp chopped fresh cilantro

- 1 Tbsp lime juice

- Sea salt

Instructions:

1. Slice the ends off the cucumbers and spiralize into flat ribbon noodles. Place in a colander, season with sea salt, and set aside.

2. Place a pot over medium high flame and heat the olive oil. Sauté the onion and curry powder until the onion is translucent.

3. Stir in the chicken stock, 1/4 teaspoon of salt, and coconut milk. Increase heat to a simmer, then add the halibut fillets.

4. Spoon the sauce over the fillets, then cover the pan and cook for about 6 minutes or until the halibut is cooked through.

5. Take the halibut out of the sauce using a slotted spatula, then place on a platter and cover to keep warm.

6. Rinse the zucchini noodles, then blot dry using paper towels.

7. Add the lime juice and cilantro into the sauce, then add the zucchini noodles and cook for about 5 minutes or until noodles are al dente.

8. Divide the sauce between two deep dishes, then place a halibut over each and serve.

Carrot and Garlic Pasta

Makes: 2 servings

Ingredients:

- 2 large carrots, peeled
- 2 Tbsp gluten free tahini paste
- 2 Tbsp olive oil
- 2 tsp grated fresh ginger
- 2 tsp tamari
- 2 garlic cloves, grated
- 6 Tbsp freshly squeezed lemon juice
- 2 tsp pine nuts

Instructions:

1. In a bowl, combine the tahini, olive oil, ginger,, tamari, garlic, and lemon juice very well. Set aside.

2. Slice the ends off the carrots and spiralize them into spaghetti noodles.

3. Add the sauce on top of the carrots, then toss to coat.

4. Divide the pasta into two servings, then sprinkle the pine nuts on top and serve at once.

Stir Fried Pork with Cabbage Noodles

Makes: 2 servings

Ingredients:

- 1/2 lb organic lean ground pork

- 3 scallions, white and green parts, chopped

- 1 small carrot, peeled and julienned

- 1/2 tsp grated ginger

- 1/2 small cabbage, cored, outer leaves discarded

- 1/2 red bell pepper, seeded and julienned

- 2 garlic cloves, minced

- 1/2 Tbsp coconut aminos

- 1 Tbsp rice vinegar

- 1/8 tsp chili oil

- 1 Tbsp arrowroot powder

- 1 Tbsp freshly squeezed orange juice

Instructions:

1. Spiralize the cabbage into thin, flat noodles. Set aside.

2. Place a wok or sauté pan over medium high flame and add the pork. Cook until browned and crumbled, then transfer to a platter using a slotted spoon and set aside.

3. In the same wok or pan, stir fry the ginger, scallions, bell pepper, carrot, and cabbage noodles for about 5 minutes.

4. Stir in the garlic and sauté for about half a minute.

5. Scrape the cooked ground pork back into the pan and stir fry everything to combine.

6. In a bowl, combine the chili oil, rice vinegar, coconut aminos, arrowroot powder, and orange juice.

7. Drizzle the sauce into the wok or pan and stir fry everything for about 3 minutes. Transfer to a platter and serve warm.

Moroccan Zu Cauli Meatballs

Makes: 4 servings

Ingredients:

- 2 medium heads cauliflower, chopped
- 4 Tbsp olive oil
- 8 garlic cloves, peeled
- 1 tsp freshly ground black pepper
- 1 tsp ground anise seeds
- 2 tsp cumin
- 1 tsp cinnamon
- 2 tsp ground cardamom
- Juice and grated zest of 2 limes
- 6 large zucchini
- 1/2 cup grated nut cheese, Parmesan substitute
- Sea salt

Instructions:

1. Set the oven to 375 degrees F to preheat.

2. Combine half of the cauliflower and peeled garlic cloves in a baking sheet and drizzle half the olive oil all over. Toss to coat, then roast for

about 20 minutes, or until garlic is fragrant and cauliflower is golden brown.

3. Set the roasted cauliflower and garlic on a wire rack to cool to room temperature. Do not turn off the oven heat.

4. Place the remaining cauliflower in a food processor and pulse until grainy. Add some salt and pulse again to combine.

5. Transfer the processed cauliflower to a saucepan with water and place over high flame. Bring to a boil, then set heat to low and let simmer for about 10 minutes, or until water is almost completely evaporated. Set aside and cool to room temperature.

6. Chop the roasted garlic and cauliflower until pasty. Place in a bowl and stir in the boiled cauliflower, then season with the black pepper and a teaspoon of salt.

7. In another bowl, mix together the cumin, anise, cinnamon, and cardamom. Use half of the mixture to season the cauliflower mixture.

8. Stir the lime juice and zest into the cauliflower mixture, then slowly drizzle the olive oil into the mixture as you stir.

9. Grease a baking sheet with some olive oil and set aside.

10. Divide the cauliflower mixture into 1 inch balls, then arrange the pieces on the prepared baking sheet. Bake for 20 minutes, or until golden brown and crisp.

11. Slice the ends off the zucchini and spiralize into extra thin noodles. Heat the remaining olive oil in a small saucepan, then stir in with the remaining spice mixture. Add the zucchini noodles and season to taste with salt. Cook for about 3 minutes, or until zucchini noodles are al dente.

12. Add the cauliflower balls into the saucepan and toss gently to combine. Divide into individual servings, then top with the nut cheese and serve.

Summer Squash Coconut Carbonara

Makes: 2 servings

Ingredients:

- 3 yellow summer squash

- 1 1/2 Tbsp olive oil

- 1 Tbsp heavy coconut cream

- 1 egg, beaten

- 2 garlic cloves, minced

- 2 oz pancetta, diced

- 1/2 shallot, minced

- 3 oz Paleo-friendly nut cheese, grated

- 1/8 tsp freshly ground black pepper

- 1 Tbsp chopped fresh flat leaf parsley

- Crushed red pepper flakes

Instructions:

1. Slice the ends off the summer squash, then spiralize them into spaghetti noodles. Set aside.

2. Place a sauté pan over medium high flame and heat the olive oil. Add the pancetta and

shallots and cook for about 5 minutes or until pancetta becomes browned.

3. Stir in the garlic and cook for half a minute, then stir in the squash noodles and sauté for about 3 minutes or until the noodles are al dente.

4. In a bowl, beat the egg together with the nut cheese, coconut cream, pepper, and a dash of red pepper flakes. Pour the mixture with the hot noodles and stir until eggs are cooked.

5. Add the parsley and serve at once.

Spaghetti with Meatballs

Makes: 2 servings

Ingredients:

- 2 zucchini
- 1 1/2 Tbsp olive oil
- Sea salt

For the Sauce:

- 1 Tbsp olive oil
- 1/2 shallot, minced
- 14 oz canned crushed tomatoes, undrained
- 1/2 Tbsp dried oregano
- 1/2 Tbsp dried basil
- 1/4 tsp sea salt
- 1/4 tsp freshly ground black pepper
- 1/16 tsp crushed red pepper flakes
- 2 garlic cloves, minced

For the Meatballs:

- 1/4 lb ground beef, grass fed
- 1/4 lb organic lean ground pork
- 2 garlic cloves, minced

- 1/4 cup almond meal

- 1 small egg, beaten

- 1 Tbsp minced shallot

- 1/2 Tbsp Italian seasoning

Instructions:

1. Slice the ends off the zucchini and spiralize into spaghetti noodles. Place the zucchini noodles in a colander and season with salt. Set aside for at least half an hour.

2. Rinse and pat the noodles dry using paper towels, then set aside.

3. Set the oven to 400 degrees F to preheat. Prepare a baking sheet by lining it with parchment paper.

4. In a bowl, combine the beef, pork, garlic, almond meal, shallot, Italian seasoning, and egg using clean hands. Divide the mixture into inch sized balls and arrange them on the baking sheet.

5. Bake the meatballs for 25 minutes, or until cooked through. Turn off the oven heat and let the meatballs stand inside until ready to serve.

6. To make the sauce, place a saucepan over medium high flame and heat the olive oil. Stir in the shallot and cook until tender. Stir in the garlic and cook for half a minute or until fragrant.

7. Stir in the tomatoes with their juices, red pepper flakes, salt, pepper, basil, and oregano. Reduce to medium low flame and add the zucchini noodles. Let simmer for about 4 minutes or until the zucchini noodles are al dente.

8. Divide the spaghetti into two servings, then take out the meatballs from the oven. Divide the meatballs between the two servings, then serve.

Chapter 10 – Salads II

Greek Salad with Zucchini Noodles

Makes: 2 servings

Ingredients:

- 2 Tbsp freshly squeezed lemon juice
- 1/2 Tbsp olive oil
- 1/2 Tbsp balsamic vinegar
- 1/2 tsp minced fresh oregano
- Sea salt
- Freshly ground black pepper
- 1 large zucchini, peeled
- 1/2 cup halved cherry or grape tomatoes
- 1/4 cup halved pitted kalamata olives
- Optional: crumbled feta cheese

Instructions:

1. In a bowl, combine the balsamic vinegar, olive oil, lemon juice, and oregano. Season to taste with salt and pepper, then set aside.

2. Slice the ends off the zucchini and spiralize into flat noodles. Place in a bowl, then toss in the olives, tomatoes, and feta cheese, if using. Drizzle the dressing all over the salad, then toss to coat and serve at once.

Citrus Strawberry and Cucumber Salad

Makes: 2 servings

Ingredients:

- 1 cucumber, peeled
- 1 cup baby spinach
- 1/2 pint strawberries, sliced and hulled
- Juice of 1/2 orange
- Zest of 1/4 orange
- 1/2 Tbsp apple cider vinegar
- 1/4 tsp chopped fresh thyme
- 2 Tbsp olive oil
- 1/4 tsp sea salt
- 1/8 tsp freshly ground black pepper

Instructions:

1. Slice the ends off the cucumber and spiralize into spaghetti noodles. Pat the noodles dry using paper towels, then place in a salad bowl.

2. Toss the spinach and sliced strawberries with the cucumber. Place in the refrigerator until ready to serve.

3. In a bowl, combine the apple cider vinegar, orange juice, orange zest, salt, pepper, and thyme. Gradually drizzle in the olive oil as you whisk until all of the ingredients are thoroughly combined.

4. Take the salad out of the refrigerator, then drizzle the dressing over the salad. Toss to coat, then serve.

Thai Carrot Salad with Almond Sauce

Makes: 2 servings

Ingredients:

- 3 small carrots, peeled
- 1 Tbsp creamy almond butter
- 2 Tbsp coconut milk
- 1 Tbsp liquid aminos
- 1 large garlic clove, minced
- 1/2 Tbsp freshly squeezed lime juice
- 1/2 Tbsp peeled grated fresh ginger
- 1 Tbsp minced fresh cilantro
- 2 Tbsp roasted cashews
- Sea salt

Instructions:

1. In a small bowl, combine the almond butter, coconut milk, liquid aminos, garlic, lime juice, and ginger. Season to taste with salt, then set aside.

2. Slice the ends off the carrots, then spiralize them into flat ribbon noodles. Place the

noodles into a bowl, then drizzle the sauce all over. Toss to coat.

3. Sprinkle the roasted cashews and chopped cilantro on top of the salad, then serve at once.

Festive Chicken Salad with Garlic Aioli

Makes: 2 servings

Ingredients:

- 1 large carrot, peeled
- 1/2 cup chopped broccoli florets, lightly steamed and drained
- 1/2 red bell pepper, seeded and julienned
- 1/4 fennel bulb
- 1 scallion, white and green parts, sliced thinly
- 2 cups chopped cooked boneless, skinless chicken
- Grated zest of 1/4 lemon
- 1/2 Tbsp freshly squeezed lemon juice
- 1 Tbsp chopped fresh tarragon
- 1/4 tsp sea salt
- 1/8 tsp freshly ground black pepper

For the Garlic Aioli:

- 1 garlic clove, minced
- 3 Tbsp extra virgin olive oil
- 1 egg yolk

- 1 Tbsp red wine vinegar

- 1/4 tsp Dijon mustard

- Sea salt

Instructions:

1. Slice the ends off the carrot, then spiralize into ribbon noodles. Slice the carrot ribbon noodles into 2 inch bits, then place in a salad bowl.

2. Toss the broccoli florets, bell pepper, and scallions with the carrot ribbon noodles. Shred the chicken and toss in.

3. With a vegetable peeler or mandolin, shave the fennel bulb and toss the shavings into the salad. Refrigerate the salad until ready to serve.

4. To make the aioli, combine the garlic, red wine vinegar, Dijon mustard, a dash of salt, and egg yolk in a food processor. Pulse as you slowly drizzle in the olive oil. Transfer the aioli into a sterilized jar. Excess can be stored for up to 7 days in the refrigerator.

5. In a bowl, combine the aioli, tarragon, salt, pepper, lemon juice and zest.

6. Drizzle the dressing all over the salad, then toss to coat and serve at once.

Zucchini Noodles with Avocado Sauce

Makes: 2 servings

Ingredients:

- 2 zucchini

- 2 scallions, white and green parts, sliced thinly

- 1/2 avocado, peeled and pitted

- 1 garlic clove

- Juice of 1 lime

- 2 Tbsp extra virgin olive oil

- 1/4 tsp ground cumin

- 1/2 chipotle chili in adobo sauce, minced

- 2 Tbsp vinegar

- 2 Tbsp chopped fresh cilantro

- 1/4 tsp sea salt

- Cayenne pepper

Instructions:

1. Combine the avocado, garlic, lime juice, olive oil, cumin, chipotle chili, vinegar, cilantro, sea salt, and a dash of cayenne pepper in a food

processor. Process until you get a smooth consistency.

2. Slice the ends of the zucchini and spiralize them into flat ribbon noodles. Place in a bowl, then drizzle the avocado sauce on top. Toss everything to coat.

3. Top the salad with scallions, then serve at once.

Oriental Rainbow Salad

Makes: 2 servings

Ingredients:

- 1 small carrot, peeled
- 1/2 green or red apple, cored
- 1 yellow beet, peeled
- 1 zucchini
- 2 large red radishes
- 2 Tbsp roughly chopped toasted almonds
- 1 Tbsp black sesame seeds
- 1/2 cup cooked shredded chicken
- 1/2 cup cold water
- Juice from 1/4 lemon
- 1 Tbsp extra virgin olive oil
- 1 Tbsp Japanese rice wine

Instructions:

1. Slice the ends off the carrot, beet, zucchini, and radishes, then spiralize them into flat noodles. Toss together in a salad bowl.

2. In a separate bowl, combine the cold water and lemon juice. Slice the ends off the apple

and spiralize into flat noodles. Place the apple noodles into the bowl of lemon water to prevent brown spots.

3. Meanwhile, combine the extra virgin olive oil and rice wine in a bowl. Whisk well to combine, then drizzle half over the vegetable salad and toss to coat.

4. Add the chicken, black sesame seeds, and almonds to the salad and toss.

5. Drain the apple noodles and toss with the salad. Drizzle the remaining dressing and toss. Serve at once.

Roasted Sweet Potato and Pecan Salad

Makes: 2 servings

Ingredients:

- 1 cup chopped pecans
- 1 large sweet potato, peeled
- 1 small yellow onion
- 1 Tbsp extra virgin olive oil
- 1 small garlic clove, minced
- 1/2 tsp sea salt
- 1/4 cup Paleo-friendly mayonnaise
- Juice and zest of 1/2 lemon
- 1/2 tsp thyme

Instructions:

1. Set the oven to 375 degrees F to preheat. Line a baking sheet using parchment pepper.

2. Spread the chopped pecans on the prepared baking sheet in a single layer, then roast for about 8 minutes, or until fragrant.

3. Remove the baking sheet from the oven and set on a wire rack to cool.

4. Slice the ends off the sweet potato, then spiralize into spiral ribbons and set aside. Next, peel and spiralize the onion into spiral ribbons. Place the sweet potato and onion in a large bowl. Drizzle in the olive oil and toss everything to coat.

5. Spread the salad mixture on the baking sheet and roast for 10 minutes, or until golden brown. Set on a wire rack to cool to room temperature.

6. Combine the minced garlic with the salt in a salad bowl, then stir in the lemon juice and zest, thyme, and mayonnaise. Mix very well, then stir in the pecans.

7. Add the roasted sweet potato and onion mixture then toss to coat. Serve at room temperature or chilled.

French Celery Root Salad

Makes: 2 servings

Ingredients:

- 1 large celery root or celeriac

- 1/2 Tbsp Dijon mustard

- 1/4 tsp prepared horseradish

- Grated zest and juice of 1/2 lemon

- 1/2 cup Paleo-friendly mayonnaise

- 1/4 tsp white pepper

- 1/2 tsp sea salt

- 2 Tbsp chopped fresh flat leaf parsley leaves

- 1/2 Tbsp chopped fresh chives

- 1/2 Tbsp chopped fresh tarragon

- 1/2 Tbsp chopped fresh chervil

Instructions:

1. Slice the celery root into manageable pieces, then spiralize into extra thin noodles. Slice the noodles into 2 inch bits and place in a refrigerator.

2. In a separate bowl, whip together the mayonnaise, horseradish, and Dijon mustard.

Whisk in the parsley, chives, tarragon, chervil, lemon juice and zest, and a dash of salt and pepper.

3. Pour the dressing over the salad and toss to coat. Refrigerate for at least half an hour before serving. Always serve chilled.

Sweet and Spicy Cucumber Salad

Makes: 2 servings

Ingredients:

- 2 large cucumbers
- 1/2 cup chopped arugula
- 1/4 cup cherry tomatoes, halved
- 1 Tbsp red wine vinegar
- 2 Tbsp olive oil, extra virgin
- 1/2 Tbsp raw honey
- 1/2 tsp crushed red pepper flakes
- Juice of 1/2 orange
- 1/4 tsp garlic powder
- Sea salt
- black pepper, freshly ground

Instructions:

1. Slice the ends off the cucumbers, then spiralize into flat ribbon noodles. Place the noodles in a bowl, then toss in the arugula and tomatoes. Refrigerate until ready to serve.

2. In a small bowl, combine the red wine vinegar, olive oil, honey, red pepper flakes, orange juice, and garlic powder. Season to taste

with salt and pepper, then whisk well until combined.

3. Take the salad out of the refrigerator and drizzle the dressing on top. Toss to coat, then serve at once.

Oriental Zucchini Noodle Salad

Makes: 2 servings

Ingredients:

- 1 zucchini, peeled
- 1 carrot, peeled
- 2 green onions, sliced thinly
- 1/2 red bell pepper, seeded
- 2 Tbsp canola oil
- 1/2 tsp dark sesame oil
- 2 Tbsp coconut aminos
- 2 Tbsp rice vinegar
- 1/2 tsp ginger
- 1 Tbsp fresh mint
- 1/2 tsp crushed red pepper flakes

Instructions:

1. Slice the ends off the zucchini and carrot, then spiralize into flat ribbon noodles. Transfer the noodles into a bowl.

2. Add the bell pepper and green onions to the salad, then toss to combine. Refrigerate until ready to serve.

3. In a small bowl, whisk together the canola oil, dark sesame oil, coconut aminos, rice vinegar, ginger, mint, and red pepper flakes. Set aside for 10 minutes to let the flavors meld.

4. Take the salad out of the refrigerator. Whisk the dressing again before drizzling over the salad. Toss to coat, then serve at once.

Chapter 11 - Desserts

Baked Apple Kugel

Makes: 4 servings

Ingredients:

- 2 apples, stemmed and cored

- 2 eggs

- 1/4 cup and 1 1/2 Tbsp coconut oil, melted, divided

- 1/4 cup freshly squeezed orange juice

- 1/4 tsp stevia

- 2 Tbsp tapioca flour

- 1/2 cup almond meal flour, divided

- 3/4 tsp ground cinnamon, divided

- 1/2 tsp vanilla extract

- 1/8 tsp sea salt

Instructions:

1. Set the oven to 350 degrees F to preheat. Prepare a small baking pan by coating its inside with about 1/2 tablespoon of melted coconut oil.

2. Slice the ends of the apples and spiralize into ribbon noodles. Slice the noodles into bite sized bits.

3. In a bowl, whisk the eggs, then beat in about 1/4 cup of cooled melted coconut oil, followed by the orange juice, stevia, salt, vanilla extract, tapioca flour, 1/2 teaspoon of cinnamon, and 2/3 of the almond meal.

4. Gently stir in the apple noodles, then pour the mixture into the prepared pan.

5. In a separate bowl, combine the remaining almond meal flour with the remaining cinnamon and melted coconut oil. Distribute the mixture evenly over the apple noodle mixture.

6. Bake the kugel for 40 minutes. Poke the center with a toothpick, and if it comes out clean then it is ready.

7. Set on a wire rack to cool for a few minutes before serving.

Cinnamon Carrot Pudding

Makes: 3 servings

Ingredients:

- 4 carrots, peeled

- 2 1/2 Tbsp coconut oil

- 3 Tbsp raw honey

- 4 tsp cinnamon

- 2 frozen bananas, peeled

Instructions:

1. Slice the ends off the carrots and spiralize into thin noodles. Slice into half inch bits and set aside.

2. Heat 1/4 teaspoon of coconut oil in a skillet over medium flame. Add the carrot noodles and sauté for 5 minutes, or until tender.

3. Meanwhile, combine the raw honey, 3 teaspoons of cinnamon, and the remaining coconut oil inside a saucepan. Place over very low flame and stir constantly until the ingredients are thoroughly combined.

4. Take the saucepan off the heat, then stir in the carrots. Place the saucepan over medium flame and cook, stirring constantly, for about 12 minutes or until the mixture becomes very creamy.

5. Divide among 3 bowls. Slice the frozen bananas and top the carrot pudding with the slices. Serve at once.

Banana and Carrot Muffins

Makes: 18 servings

Ingredients:

- 5 carrots, peeled
- 2 cups almond meal
- 2/3 tsp baking soda
- 1/3 tsp sea salt
- 2/3 tsp baking powder
- 2/3 tsp stevia
- 1 1/2 tsp ground ginger
- 1 1/2 Tbsp ground cinnamon
- 3 mashed extra ripe bananas
- 6 eggs
- 1/3 cup coconut milk
- 1/3 cup melted coconut oil
- 1 1/2 tsp vanilla extract

Instructions:

1. Set the oven to 350 degrees F to preheat. Prepare 18 muffin cups and line them using paper liners.

2. Slice the ends off the carrots, then spiralize them into spaghetti noodles. Slice the noodles into 2 inch bits and set aside.

3. Sift the baking powder, almond meal, baking soda, stevia, ginger, and cinnamon in a bowl. Stir in the salt.

4. In a separate bowl, combine the coconut oil, mashed bananas, vanilla extract, and coconut milk.

5. Create a pit in the center of the coconut flour mixture and pour the banana mixture in the center. Let the dry ingredients collapse into the wet ingredients, then mix everything until just combined; do not over-mix.

6. Gently mix in the carrot noodles until evenly distributed.

7. Divide the batter among the prepared muffin cups, then bake for 25 minutes. Poke the center with a toothpick, and if it comes out clean then it is ready.

8. Set on a wire rack to cool for a few minutes before serving.

Crisp Apple Cinnamon Bites

Makes: 3 servings

Ingredients:

- 1 cup almond flour

- 1 tsp baking powder

- 1/4 tsp cinnamon

- 1/2 tsp sea salt

- 1/4 cup coconut sugar

- 1 large egg

- 1/3 cup unsweetened almond milk

- 2 medium Fuji apples, peeled and cored

- 1/2 tsp vanilla extract

- Vegetable oil

Instructions:

1. In a bowl, combine the baking powder, almond flour, salt, coconut sugar, and cinnamon.

2. In another bowl, beat the egg together with the vanilla extract and milk.

3. Create a pit in the center of the flour mixture, then pour the egg mixture into it. Allow the dry ingredients to collapse into the

wet ingredients, then mix until just combined; do not over-mix.

4. Slice the ends off the apples, then spiralize into extra thin noodles. Slice the noodles into half inch bits.

5. Fold the apple noodles into the batter, then set aside for 10 minutes at room temperature.

6. Line a large platter with paper towels, then set aside.

7. Place a large, deep skillet over high flame and fill it with about an inch of vegetable oil. Use a deep fry thermometer to check if it has reached 375 degrees F, otherwise, drop a tiny amount of the batter into the oil. If it starts to sizzle at once, it is ready.

8. Set heat to medium, then use a tablespoon to drop the batter in bite-sized pieces into the oil; avoid overcrowding the pieces. Reduce heat to low if the mixture becomes brown too quickly. Cook until the pieces become golden brown, about a minute per side.

9. Use a slotted spoon to take the pieces out of the skillet, then place them on the prepared platter. Allow to drain thoroughly.

10. Serve the crisp apple cinnamon bites with coconut cream or a light dusting of coconut sugar on top, if desired.

Spiced Nutty Pear

Makes: 2 servings

Ingredients:

- 2 pears, stemmed, cored
- 1/4 tsp stevia
- 1/4 tsp ground ginger
- 1/4 tsp lemon zest
- 1/2 tsp lemon juice
- 1/4 tsp sea salt, divided
- 1/3 cup chopped walnuts
- 1 tsp cinnamon
- 2 Tbsp coconut flakes
- 2 Tbsp coconut oil, melted
- 2 Tbsp almond meal

Instructions:

1. Set the oven to 350 degrees F to preheat.

2. Slice the ends off the pears, then spiralize into flat ribbon noodles. Slice the pear noodles into 2 inch bits and place in a bowl.

3. Add the stevia, lemon juice and zest, ginger, half the salt, and 1/2 teaspoon of cinnamon to

the pear noodles. Toss everything to combine, then transfer to a small baking pan.

4. In a separate bowl, mix together the almond meal, coconut flakes, remaining salt, remaining cinnamon, walnuts, and coconut oil.

5. Distribute the walnut mixture evenly over the pear noodles.

6. Bake for about 25 minutes, or until the top of the dessert is browned and the pear is tender.

7. Set on a wire rack to cool before serving.

Choco Coco Zucchini Cookies

Makes: 6 servings

Ingredients:

- 1/2 cup almond flour
- 1/4 tsp sea salt
- 1/2 tsp baking soda
- 1/3 tsp ground cinnamon
- 2 Tbsp pureed apple
- 1 small egg
- 1/3 cup coconut sugar
- 1 small zucchini
- 1 cup coconut flakes
- 1/4 cup cacao chips

Instructions:

1. Set the oven to 350 degrees F to preheat. Prepare a baking sheet by lining it with parchment paper.

2. In a bowl, combine the baking soda, almond flour, cinnamon, and salt.

3. In a separate bowl, combine the pureed apple and coconut sugar until smooth. Whisk in the egg, followed by the vanilla extract.

4. Slice the ends of the zucchini and spiralize into extra thin noodles. Slice the noodles into half inch bits. Fold the noodles into the egg mixture.

1. Create a pit in the center of the flour mixture and pour the egg mixture in the center. Let the dry ingredients collapse into the wet ingredients, then mix everything until just combined; do not over-mix.

5. Add the cacao chips and coconut flakes to the batter. Mix carefully until evenly distributed.

6. Use a cookie scoop of a tablespoon to make cookies on the prepared baking sheet. Leave about 3 inches of space in between each cookie.

7. Bake for 10 minutes, or until the edges are pale brown. Turn off the heat and let the cookies stay in the oven for 5 minutes.

8. Transfer the cookies on a wire rack to cool before serving.

Sweet Squash Muffins

Makes: 18 servings

Ingredients:

- 1 small butternut squash, peeled

- Zest of 1 large orange

- 3/4 cup coconut flour

- 3 extra ripe banana, mashed

- 1 1/2 tsp ground cinnamon

- 1/3 cup coconut oil, melted

- 1/3 Tbsp coconut milk

- 1/3 tsp ground cloves

- 1 1/2 tsp vanilla extract

Instructions:

2. Set the oven to 350 degrees F to preheat. Prepare 18 muffin cups and line them using paper liners.

3. Slice the squash into manageable pieces, then spiralize into extra thin noodles. Slice the noodles into inch sized bits.

4. In a bowl, combine the cinnamon, cloves, coconut flour, and orange zest.

5. In a separate bowl, combine the mashed bananas, coconut milk, vanilla extract, and melted coconut oil.

6. Create a pit in the center of the coconut flour mixture and pour the banana mixture in the center. Let the dry ingredients collapse into the wet ingredients, then mix everything until just combined; do not over-mix.

7. Gently mix in the butternut squash noodles until evenly distributed.

8. Divide the batter among the prepared muffin cups, then bake for 20 minutes. Poke the center with a toothpick, and if it comes out clean then it is ready.

9. Set on a wire rack to cool for a few minutes before serving.

Conclusion

Thank you again for buying this book!

I hope this book was able to help you create delicious and nutritious meals using your spiralizer.

The next step is to prepare a meal plan that will help you include more vegetable pastas to your diet.

Finally, if you enjoyed this book, please take the time to share your thoughts and post a review on Amazon. It'd be greatly appreciated!

Thank you and good luck!

45832116R00112

Made in the USA
Lexington, KY
12 October 2015